Exercises in Management

MANAGEMENT

4th Edition

Exercises in Management

MANAGEMENT

4th Edition

Griffin

Gene E. Burton
California State University, Fresno

HOUGHTON MIFFLIN COMPANY   BOSTON   TORONTO
Dallas   Geneva, Illinois   Palo Alto   Princeton, New Jersey

Sponsoring Editor: Diane L. McOscar
Development Editor: Julie Hogenboom
Manufacturing Coordinator: Sharon Pearson

ISBN: 0-395-65851-9

123456789-PO-96 95 94 93 92

Contents

Contents

A Word to the Student

In order to learn management principles—that is, to *really* learn them—we must learn them through experience, by doing. Reading books and listening to lectures, no matter how inspiring, do not have the learning value or impact that is found in "hands-on" learning.

Because of the importance of experiential learning, this book of learning exercises is provided as a means by which the management principles can come to life and have true meaning for you. For each area of Management Principles or Management Skills, this book contains related exercises by which those principles and skills are applied to real-world situations. In this way, the student learns first hand how to apply management concepts to life and to our society.

The learning value of the exercises is increased if you try to follow a few simple rules:

1. REALLY GET INVOLVED. The more you get involved, the more you will learn.
2. Always BE YOURSELF.
3. Be HONEST.
4. Be SINCERE.
5. SHARE your ideas and experiences.
6. Allow others to give you FEEDBACK on your ideas and your contributions.
7. Try to UNDERSTAND WHAT'S GOING ON.
8. Try to RELATE EACH EXERCISE TO THE COURSE MATERIAL.

Good luck and good learning!

CHAPTER 1   MANAGING AND THE MANAGER'S JOB

Exercise 1.1—Who's a Manager?

PURPOSE

Help identify managers and managerial functions

TIME REQUIRED

45 minutes

    Step 1: Individual activity (10 minutes)
    Step 2: Small-group activity (20 minutes)
    Step 3: Class discussion (15 minutes)

MATERIALS NEEDED

None

PROCEDURE

Step 1: Students should consider each of the following positions and decide whether each is a manager or not, giving at least one reason for the answer.

Position	A Manager? Yes	A Manager? No	Reason
Teacher	_____	_____	_____
Policeman	_____	_____	_____
Surgeon	_____	_____	_____
Homemaker	_____	_____	_____
Football Coach	_____	_____	_____
Church Custodian	_____	_____	_____

Step 2: The instructor will divide the class into small groups and assign one of the above positions to each group and ask each group to identify any activities related to that position that can be considered functions of management.

Position Assigned: ———————————

Management Function	**Activity**
Planning and Decision Making	

Organizing

Leading

Controlling

Step 3: One representative from each group should present the group's findings and the group's responses to the discussion questions to the class.

QUESTIONS FOR DISCUSSION

1. Can you identify someone who is not a manager? Why is that person not a manager?
2. Is everyone a manager? Why or why not?
3. Where and how do some of these managers develop managerial skills?

Exercise 1.2—Organizational Resources

PURPOSE

Help identify the variety of resources used by organizations

TIME REQUIRED

45 minutes

    Step 1: Individual activity (10 minutes)

    Step 2: Small-group activity (20 minutes)

    Step 3: Class discussion (15 minutes)

MATERIALS NEEDED

None

PROCEDURE

Step 1: Students should consider each of the following organizations on p. 5 and list under the appropriate categories the resources they use.

Step 2: The instructor will divide the class into small groups, assigning each group to one of the organizations. The group should develop a master list of the resources used by that organization. The group should also develop responses to the discussion questions.

Step 3: One representative from each group should present the group's findings to the class.

QUESTIONS FOR DISCUSSION

1. Are there some resources used by all organizations?
2. Can you think of an organization that does not use one of the resource categories?
3. Which functional managers are responsible for different kinds of resources?

Organization	Human Resources	Financial Resources	Physical Resources	Information Resources
A State University				
Bank of America				
Macy's				
General Motors				
County Hospital				
Independent Gasoline Station				

Student's Name

5

Exercise 1.3—Managerial Role Questionnaire (MRQ)

PURPOSE

Help students understand the nature of managerial roles and their own role tendencies

TIME REQUIRED

45 minutes

    Step 1: Individual activity (15 minutes)

    Step 2: Small-group activity (15 minutes)

    Step 3: Class discussion (15 minutes)

MATERIALS NEEDED

None

PROCEDURE

Step 1: Henry Mintzberg writes that if groups are to reach goals, certain managerial roles must be filled. This questionnaire is designed to measure the degree to which students perceive themselves as filling those managerial roles. Students should think back to group situations in which they have participated and indicate their perception of their behavior by circling the appropriate number on the scale for each statement on p. 9. Then they should score the instrument following the instructions on the scoring sheet on p. 10.

Step 2: The instructor will divide the class into small groups. Each group should compute the group's average scores, analyze the difference in individual scores, and develop group responses to the discussion questions.

Step 3: The instructor may collect the groups' average scores in order to compute class-average scores. Group representatives can then respond to the discussion questions.

QUESTIONS FOR DISCUSSION

1. In what areas are the scores more in agreement? Less in agreement? Why?
2. What might account for some of the differences in individual or group scores?
3. How can the results of this exercise be put to constructive use?

Managerial Role Questionnaire

Statement	Strongly Agree	Slightly Agree	Not Sure	Slightly Disagree	Strongly Disagree
1. When visitors come to our group, I am active in greeting them.	5	4	3	2	1
2. When I'm given the responsibility for a group activity, I work hard to motivate those assigned to the task.	5	4	3	2	1
3. When appropriate, I give talks or speeches in order to inform others.	5	4	3	2	1
4. I tend to be the group's representative in cases of conflict and dispute.	5	4	3	2	1
5. When a group member complains to me, I try to resolve the complaint.	5	4	3	2	1
6. I believe in distributing group resources on the basis of demonstrated need.	5	4	3	2	1
7. I tend to develop useful contacts outside the group.	5	4	3	2	1
8. I encourage meetings and memos to improve communication.	5	4	3	2	1
9. I devote time and effort to finding out what's going on outside the group.	5	4	3	2	1
10. I welcome new ideas and new ways of thinking.	5	4	3	2	1
11. I believe in talking through issues in order to achieve satisfactory agreements.	5	4	3	2	1
12. I enjoy the task of coordinating two work groups.	5	4	3	2	1
13. I am active in providing information to people outside the group.	5	4	3	2	1
14. If a group member got married, I would attend the wedding.	5	4	3	2	1
15. I'll change procedures if I think they will improve group performance.	5	4	3	2	1
16. When I'm in charge of a group activity, I tend to work closely with those doing the work.	5	4	3	2	1
17. I believe that requests for resources should be accompanied with an appropriate budget.	5	4	3	2	1
18. Information is power, and I work hard to collect information important to the group.	5	4	3	2	1
19. When there is conflict, I resolve it quickly.	5	4	3	2	1
20. If I come across information that is important, I share it with the group.	5	4	3	2	1

Managerial Role Questionnaire Scoring Sheet

Transfer your numeric responses from the questionnaire onto this scoring sheet and sum the items to find your score(s). For example, your Figurehead score is the sum of your responses to questions 1 and 14.

Category	Roles	Items	Your Score	Your Totals
Interpersonal Roles	Figurehead	1 + 14 = _____		
	Leader	2 + 16 = _____		
	Liaison	7 + 12 = _____		_____
Informational Roles	Monitor	9 + 18 = _____		
	Disseminator	8 + 20 = _____		
	Spokesperson	3 + 13 = _____		_____
Decisional Roles	Entrepreneur	10 + 15 = _____		
	Disturbance Handler	5 + 19 = _____		
	Resource Allocator	6 + 17 = _____		
	Negotiator	4 + 11 = _____		_____

CHAPTER 2   THE EVOLUTION OF MANAGEMENT

Exercise 2.1—Theory X–Theory Y Questionnaire

PURPOSE

Help students understand McGregor's Theory X–Theory Y concept and help them clarify their own attitudes toward work and management

TIME REQUIRED

45 minutes

    Step 1: Individual activity (completed before class)

    Step 2: Small-group activity (30 minutes)

    Step 3: Class discussion (15 minutes)

MATERIALS NEEDED

None

PROCEDURE

Step 1:   Each student should complete the Theory X–Theory Y Questionnaire (p. 13) and score it in accordance with the Theory X–Theory Y Scoring Sheet (p. 14).

Step 2:   The instructor will divide the class into small groups. Each group should: (1) compute the group's average scores for both Theory X and Theory Y, (2) analyze the differences in individual scores, (3) compare responses to the questionnaire statements, and (4) develop group responses to the discussion questions.

Step 3:   The instructor may collect the groups' average scores in order to compute class-average scores. Group representatives can then respond to the discussion questions.

QUESTIONS FOR DISCUSSION

1. What might account for some of the differences in individual scores?
2. Is it possible for a person to be somewhat Theory X and somewhat Theory Y?
3. How does it feel to have a Theory X or a Theory Y label placed on you?

Theory X–Theory Y Questionnaire

Statement	Strongly Agree	Slightly Agree	Not Sure	Slightly Disagree	Strongly Disagree
1. Most people do not like to work.	5	4	3	2	1
2. Given the chance to think for themselves, most people are bright.	5	4	3	2	1
3. People are internally motivated to achieve goals to which they are committed.	5	4	3	2	1
4. To get work done, managers must control employees.	5	4	3	2	1
5. Above all, workers want security.	5	4	3	2	1
6. If treated properly, people will accept responsibility.	5	4	3	2	1
7. People prefer that someone else tell them what to do on the job.	5	4	3	2	1
8. Workers may have to be coerced to get things done properly.	5	4	3	2	1
9. Work is as natural as play.	5	4	3	2	1
10. Workers can be creative on the job.	5	4	3	2	1
11. At work, people show little ambition.	5	4	3	2	1
12. Some people won't work unless threatened.	5	4	3	2	1
13. Some workers will pursue goals if rewarded.	5	4	3	2	1
14. Most employees avoid work whenever possible.	5	4	3	2	1
15. Most employers don't use the full potential of their employees.	5	4	3	2	1
16. Given the chance, some workers can be innovative problem solvers.	5	4	3	2	1
17. People usually avoid responsibility.	5	4	3	2	1
18. To achieve group goals, superiors must direct the activities of their subordinates.	5	4	3	2	1
19. Under proper conditions, people will seek responsibility.	5	4	3	2	1
20. It is not natural for people to dislike work.	5	4	3	2	1

Theory X–Theory Y Scoring Sheet

Transfer your numeric responses from the questionnaire onto this scoring sheet. Then place your two total Theory X and Theory Y scores on the appropriate continuum.

Theory X Questions			Theory Y Questions		
Number		*Score*	*Number*		*Score*
1	=	_____	2	=	_____
4	=	_____	3	=	_____
5	=	_____	6	=	_____
7	=	_____	9	=	_____
8	=	_____	10	=	_____
11	=	_____	13	=	_____
12	=	_____	15	=	_____
14	=	_____	16	=	_____
17	=	_____	19	=	_____
18	=	_____	20	=	_____
Total X Score _____			Total Y Score _____		

Theory X
Continuum 50   40   30   20   10   0

Theory Y
Continuum 50   40   30   20   10   0

Exercise 2.2—Applying Management Theory

PURPOSE

Help students gain a deeper understanding of the earlier management theories (classical, behavioral, and quantitative)

TIME REQUIRED

45 minutes

Step 1: Individual activity (10 minutes)

Step 2: Small-group activity (20 minutes)

Step 3: Class discussion (15 minutes)

MATERIALS NEEDED

None

PROCEDURE

Step 1:   Each student should study Figure 2.4, An Integrative Framework of Management Theories, and review the text materials on the classical management perspective, the behavior management perspective, and the quantitative management perspective. Then each student should read The Problem Situation, which follows.

THE PROBLEM SITUATION

Every year the State University's Marketing Club conducts one major fundraising project to pay for the annual Homecoming Marketing Club Bash. Last year, it seems that Murphy's Law dominated both the fundraiser and the Bash. First, the fundraiser—a calendar sale—failed to raise the required funds. The project was poorly planned, and when things started to go badly, most of the club members became discouraged and stopped selling the calendars. As a result, the club was unable to pay all the bills incurred for the Bash. In an effort to economize, they down scaled several of the Bash expenditures. For instance, the Bash had a history of always providing live bands, but that year they had to settle for recorded music. The normal buffet was reduced to chips and dip. Thus, both the fundraiser and the Bash were failures, and the club wound up over $200 in debt and in the Dean's doghouse.

A club committee has decided that in order to raise enough money to pay off their debt and properly fund this year's Bash, they will conduct a flea market. They have been making lists of the tasks to be done—advertising, goods collections, storage, pricing, location, display, selling, and so on.

Pat Malloy has just been elected president of the Marketing Club. The faculty advisor, Professor Proctor, is very unhappy over last year's failure and has informed Pat that a repeat of last year will not be tolerated. So a very worried Pat is trying to figure out ways to make sure this year's fundraiser will be a success.

Recognition of system and subsystem interdependencies,
environmental influences, and the situational nature of management

```
┌─────────────────┐   ┌─────────────────┐   ┌─────────────────┐
│ Classical       │   │ Behavioral      │   │ Quantitative    │
│ management      │   │ management      │   │ management      │
│ perspectives    │   │ perspectives    │   │ perspectives    │
│                 │   │                 │   │                 │
│ Current concerns│   │ Current concerns│   │ Current concerns│
│ for efficiency  │   │ for organizational│ │ for management  │
│ and productivity│   │ behavior        │   │ science models  │
│                 │   │                 │   │ and operations  │
│                 │   │                 │   │ management      │
└────────┬────────┘   └────────┬────────┘   └────────┬────────┘
         │                     │                     │
         ▼                     ▼                     ▼
┌──────────────────────────────────────────────────────────────┐
│                    The systems approach                        │
├──────────────────────────────────────────────────────────────┤
│                  The contingency approach                      │
└──────────────────────────────┬───────────────────────────────┘
                               ▼
┌──────────────────────────────────────────────────────────────┐
│              Effective and efficient management                │
└──────────────────────────────────────────────────────────────┘
```

FIGURE 2.4
An Integrative Framework of Management Theories (Reprinted from Ricky Griffin,
Management, 3rd ed., copyright © Houghton Mifflin Company 1990. Used by permission.)

Step 2:   The instructor will divide the class into small groups and assign each group with the tasks of
(1) completing The Problem Situation Response Sheet on p. 17, and (2) developing group responses to
the discussion questions.

Step 3:   One representative from each group should present the group's findings and the group's responses to the discussion questions.

QUESTIONS FOR DISCUSSION

1. Did some of the statements seem to reflect more than a single management perspective? Does that minimize their categorical value?
2. Can the systems approach to management be helpful to Pat? How?
3. Can the contingency approach to management be helpful to Pat? How?

The Problem Situation Response Sheet

For each statement below, indicate which management perspective it best represents.

Statement	Classical Management	Behavioral Management	Quantitative Management
1. Pat should let the committee use its own creativity.	———	———	———
2. Pat should find someone who has conducted a flea market and find out how it should be done.	———	———	———
3. Pat should see that each worker receives instruction on how to do his/her job.	———	———	———
4. Pat should do a market analysis to determine whether the area can support another flea market.	———	———	———
5. Pat should develop an inventory control system on her PC.	———	———	———
6. Pat should delegate full responsibility to each worker.	———	———	———
7. Pat should offer cash awards to those who exceed their collection or sales quotas.	———	———	———
8. Pat should use club pride to motivate the members.	———	———	———
9. Pat should develop a flow chart of the operation.	———	———	———
10. Pat should assign workers to tasks according to their skills.	———	———	———
11. Pat should require each work team to prepare a flexible budget/work schedule.	———	———	———
12. Pat should not try to control the work groups too closely.	———	———	———

17

Exercise 2.3—Organizations as Systems

PURPOSE

Help students clarify the systems approach to management by applying it to organizations with which they are familiar

TIME REQUIRED

45 minutes

    Step 1: Individual activity (10 minutes)

    Step 2: Small-group activity (20 minutes)

    Step 3: Class discussion (15 minutes)

MATERIALS NEEDED

None

PROCEDURE

Step 1: Each student should study Figure 2.3, The Systems View of Organizations, and the text materials on the systems approach to management. Then each student should apply that approach to complete the Organizational Systems Model for the five specified organizations on p. 21.

Step 2: The instructor will divide the class into small groups, assigning each group one of the five organizations. The group will develop a master Organizational Systems Model for that organization and will develop group responses to the discussion questions.

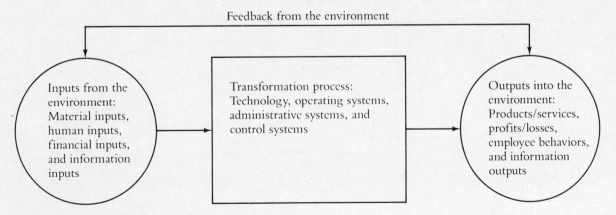

FIGURE 2.3
The Systems View of Organizations (Reprinted from Ricky Griffin, *Management*, 3rd ed., copyright © Houghton Mifflin Company 1990. Used by permission.)

Organization Assigned: _____

Inputs	Transformation Processes	Outputs
_____	_____	_____
_____	_____	_____
_____	_____	_____
_____	_____	_____
_____	_____	_____
_____	_____	_____
_____	_____	_____
_____	_____	_____
_____	_____	_____
_____	_____	_____
_____	_____	_____
_____	_____	_____

Step 3:   One representative from each group should present the group's findings and the group's responses to the discussion.

QUESTIONS FOR DISCUSSION

1. Are there some inputs that are used by most organizations?
2. Are there some transformation processes that are used by most organizations?
3. Are there some outputs that are produced by most organizations?

The Organizational Systems Model

Organization	Inputs	Transformation Processes	Outputs
Public Library	_____	_____	_____
	_____	_____	_____
	_____	_____	_____
	_____	_____	_____
	_____	_____	_____
Walmart	_____	_____	_____
	_____	_____	_____
	_____	_____	_____
	_____	_____	_____
Burger King	_____	_____	_____
	_____	_____	_____
	_____	_____	_____
	_____	_____	_____
Mattel Toys	_____	_____	_____
	_____	_____	_____
	_____	_____	_____
	_____	_____	_____
Standard Oil	_____	_____	_____
	_____	_____	_____
	_____	_____	_____
	_____	_____	_____
	_____	_____	_____

CHAPTER 3 THE ORGANIZATIONAL ENVIRONMENT AND EFFECTIVENESS

Exercise 3.1—The State University's General Environment

PURPOSE

Help students gain an understanding of the general organizational environments and the complexity of those environments for the state university

TIME REQUIRED

45 minutes

    Step 1: Individual activity (10 minutes)

    Step 2: Small-group activity (20 minutes)

    Step 3: Class discussion (15 minutes)

MATERIALS NEEDED

None

PROCEDURE

Step 1: Each student should first study Figure 3.1, The Organization and Its Environments, and Figure 3.2, Ford's General Environment, and then complete The State University General Environment Worksheet, on page 27.

Step 2: The instructor will divide the class into small groups and ask each group to develop a master State University General Environment Worksheet and to develop group responses to the discussion questions.

Step 3: The instructor may wish to create a master State University General Environment Worksheet on the chalkboard, using input from the group representatives. Group representatives can then present group responses to the discussion questions.

QUESTIONS FOR DISCUSSION

1. Which of the general environment factors appear to have the greatest impact on the top university administrators? The business school? The faculty? The educational support staff? The dean of students? The athletic department?

2. Which of the general environment factors are the most important?

3. How does the university's general environment differ from that of Ford Motor Company?

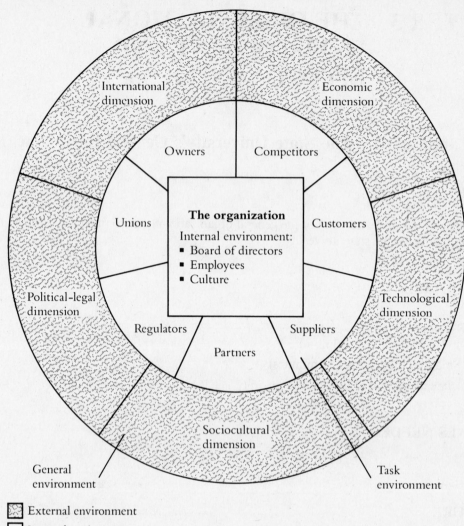

FIGURE 3.1
The Organization and Its Environments (Reprinted from Ricky Griffin, *Management,* 3rd ed., p. 80. Copyright © Houghton Mifflin Company 1990. Used by permission.)

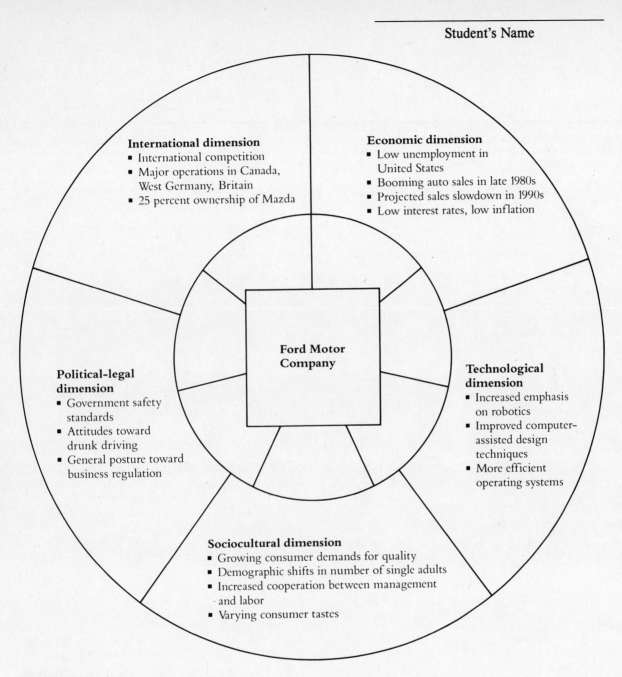

International dimension
- International competition
- Major operations in Canada, West Germany, Britain
- 25 percent ownership of Mazda

Economic dimension
- Low unemployment in United States
- Booming auto sales in late 1980s
- Projected sales slowdown in 1990s
- Low interest rates, low inflation

Political-legal dimension
- Government safety standards
- Attitudes toward drunk driving
- General posture toward business regulation

Ford Motor Company

Technological dimension
- Increased emphasis on robotics
- Improved computer-assisted design techniques
- More efficient operating systems

Sociocultural dimension
- Growing consumer demands for quality
- Demographic shifts in number of single adults
- Increased cooperation between management and labor
- Varying consumer tastes

FIGURE 3.2
Ford's General Environment (Reprinted from Ricky Griffin, *Management,* 3rd ed., p. 82. Copyright © Houghton Mifflin Company 1990. Used by permission.)

The State University General Environment Worksheet

International Dimension

_____
_____
_____
_____
_____
_____
_____
_____
_____

Economic Dimension

_____
_____
_____
_____
_____
_____
_____
_____

Political-Legal Dimension

_____
_____
_____
_____
_____
_____
_____
_____
_____

**THE STATE
UNIVERSITY**

Technological Dimension

_____
_____
_____
_____
_____
_____
_____
_____

Sociocultural Dimension

_____
_____
_____
_____
_____
_____
_____
_____

Exercise 3.2—The State University's Task Environment

PURPOSE

Help students gain an understanding of organizational task environments and the complexity of those environments for the state university

TIME REQUIRED

45 minutes

    Step 1: Individual activity (10 minutes)

    Step 2: Small-group activity (20 minutes)

    Step 3: Class discussion (15 minutes)

MATERIALS NEEDED

None

PROCEDURE

Step 1:   Each student should first study Figure 3.1, The Organization and Its Environments (see Exercise 3.1, p. 24), and Figure 3.3, Ford's Task Environment, and then complete The State University Task Environment Worksheet on page 31.

Step 2:   The instructor will divide the class into small groups and ask each group to develop a master State University Task Environment Worksheet and to develop group responses to the discussion questions.

Step 3:   The instructor may wish to create a master State University Task Environment Worksheet on the chalkboard, using input from the group representatives. Group representatives can then present group responses to the discussion questions.

QUESTIONS FOR DISCUSSION

1. Which of the task environment factors appear to have the greatest impact on the top university administrators? The business school? The faculty? The educational support staff? The dean of students? The athletic department?

2. Which of the task environment factors are the most important?

3. How does the university's task environment differ from that of Ford Motor Company?

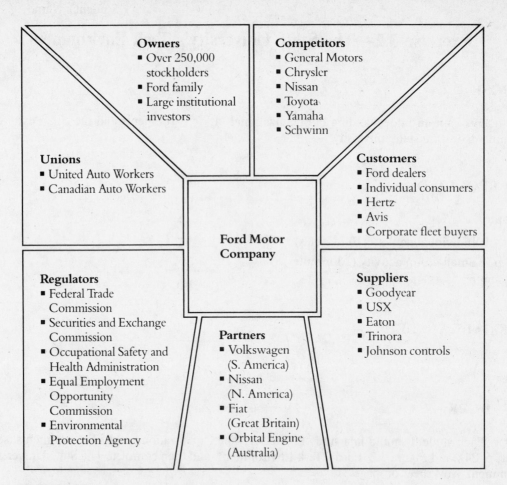

FIGURE 3.3
Ford's Task Environment (Reprinted from Ricky Griffin, *Management,* 3rd ed., p. 86. Copyright © Houghton Mifflin Company 1990. Used by permission.)

The State University Task Environment Worksheet

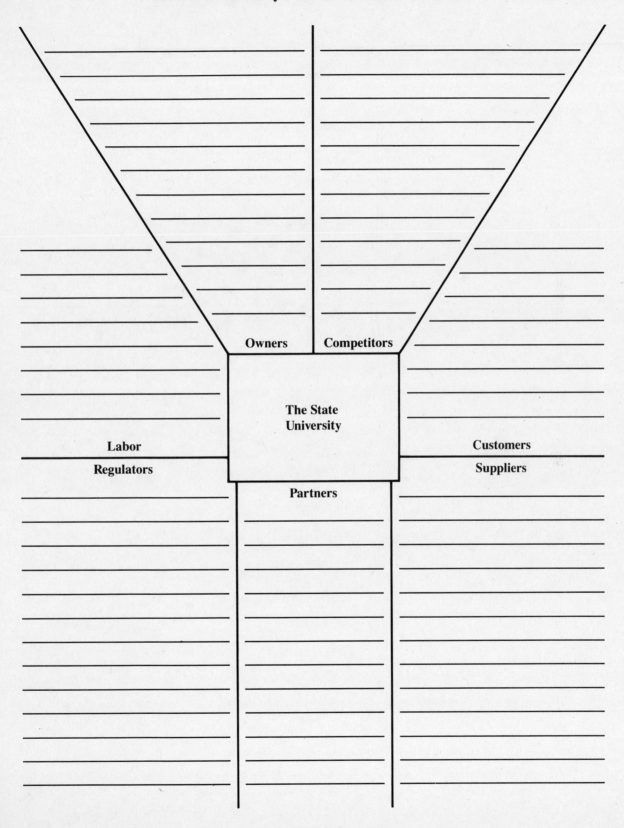

Owners   Competitors

The State University

Labor   Customers

Regulators   Suppliers

Partners

Reprinted from Ricky Griffin, *Management,* 3rd ed., copyright © Houghton Mifflin Company 1990. Used by permission.

Exercise 3.3—Environmental Change, Complexity, and Uncertainty

PURPOSE

Help students gain an understanding of the relationships between environmental change, complexity, and uncertainty

TIME REQUIRED

45 minutes

Step 1: Individual activity (10 minutes)

Step 2: Small-group activity (20 minutes)

Step 3: Class discussion (15 minutes)

MATERIALS NEEDED

None

PROCEDURE

Step 1:   Each student should study Figure 3.4, Environmental Change, Complexity, and Uncertainty and review the text material regarding this figure. Then the student should properly position the twelve companies in the matrix on The Environmental Change, Complexity, and Uncertainty Worksheet on p. 35.

Step 2:   The instructor will divide the class into small groups and assign each group to develop a group response to (1) The Environmental Change, Complexity, and Uncertainty Worksheet, and (2) the discussion questions.

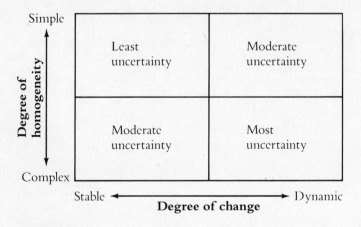

FIGURE 3.4
Environmental Change, Complexity, and Uncertainty (From J. D. Thompson, *Organizations in Action,* copyright 1967. Reprinted by permission of McGraw-Hill Book Company.)

Step 3:   The instructor may wish to develop a master Environmental Change, Complexity, and Uncertainty Worksheet on the chalkboard, using input from the group representatives. Then the group representatives can provide group input on the discussion questions.

QUESTIONS FOR DISCUSSION

1. Were some firms easier to place on the worksheet than others? Why?
2. Which of the four quadrants presents the greatest management challenge? The least?
3. Which of the four quadrants would you prefer for your career?

The Environmental Change, Complexity, and Uncertainty Worksheet

Consider the following twelve companies and place them in the proper position in the matrix below:

U.S. Steel Corporation	Toys 'R' Us
General Electric	Domino's Pizza
The Singer Company	Apple Computer, Inc.
Reebok's	Beech Aircraft Corporation
Black & Decker	Shell Oil Company
Revlon	Campbell Soup Company

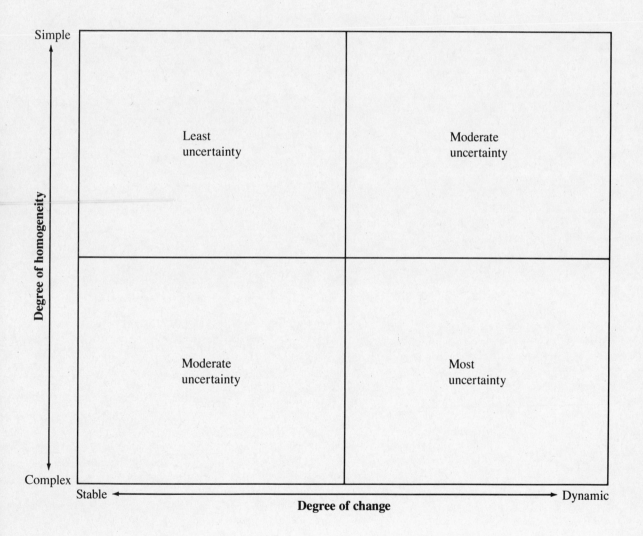

CHAPTER 4   THE ETHICAL AND SOCIAL CONTEXT OF MANAGEMENT

Exercise 4.1—Social Responsibility Versus Social Irresponsibility

PURPOSE

Help students understand the pros and cons in the continuing controversy over the social responsibility of business

TIME REQUIRED

45 minutes

> Step 1: Small-group research activity (completed before class)
> Step 2: Class discussion (45 minutes)

MATERIALS NEEDED

None

PROCEDURE

Step 1:   The instructor will divide the class into small groups for the purpose of preparing for a debate on the continuing controversy regarding the social responsibility of business. In brief, the controversy centers on whether a business has an obligation to use its resources to serve the interests of external publics.

Each group will be assigned one or more of the arguments for or against this definition of social responsibility.

ARGUMENTS FOR SOCIAL RESPONSIBILITY

1. Actions of social responsibility will enhance the company's *public image.*
2. Socially responsible behavior meets *public expectations.*
3. A socially responsible company will avoid unnecessary *government regulation/intervention.*
4. Business should take care of social issues because *business has the resources.*
5. Social responsibility will *improve the environment* for all concerned.
6. Business has a great deal of social power, so there is a need to *balance power with responsibility.*
7. Investment to improve society is in the *long-term best interests of the firm.*
8. Socially responsible behaviors are the *ethical* things to do.

ARGUMENTS AGAINST SOCIAL RESPONSIBILITY

1. Using its resources for the public good *dilutes the purpose* of the business.
2. Social responsibility behaviors will *weaken profitability.*
3. Social responsibility is in *conflict with stockholder responsibility.*
4. Socially responsible actions can be very *costly.*
5. Companies can engage in social influence *without accountability* to the people they are affecting.
6. Businesses *do not have the skills* for dealing with social problems.
7. Given the amount of power possessed by businesses, social responsibility programs would give them *too much power* over society.
8. Social responsibility programs may be *illegal.*
9. Social responsibility would lead to *dangerous business–government collusion.*

Each group should go to the library and research material in support of its argument(s).

Step 2:   The instructor should preside over the classroom social responsibility debate.

Exercise 4.2—Ethics Questionnaire

PURPOSE

Help students gain a better appreciation for the complexity of differentiating between ethical and unethical behavior

TIME REQUIRED

45 minutes

    Step 1: Individual activity (15 minutes)
    Step 2: Small-group activity (20 minutes)
    Step 3: Class discussion (10 minutes)

MATERIALS NEEDED

None

PROCEDURE

Step 1: Each student should complete and score The Ethics Questionnaire (pp. 41–42).

Step 2: Each group should compute its average scores and develop group responses to the discussion questions.

Step 3: A representative from each group will present the group's findings for class discussion.

QUESTIONS FOR DISCUSSION

1. Was there greater agreement on Managerial Ethics Scores or on Employee Ethics Scores? Why?
2. What might account for differences of opinions on the definition of ethical behavior?
3. How can the results of this questionnaire be put to constructive use?

The Ethics Questionnaire

Statement	Strongly Agree	Slightly Agree	Not Sure	Slightly Disagree	Strongly Disagree
1. It's OK for management to pay for lavish entertainment to land a big contract.	1	2	3	4	5
2. It's OK for a worker to falsify his/her time card when late to work.	1	2	3	4	5
3. A manager should not use a company car for personal use.	5	4	3	2	1
4. A worker should not call in sick to get an extra day off.	5	4	3	2	1
5. For management, the goal-achievement end usually justifies the means used.	1	2	3	4	5
6. A worker may use the office copier to copy personal documents.	1	2	3	4	5
7. It is wrong for management to give gifts/favors in exchange for favors that help the firm.	5	4	3	2	1
8. A worker should not conduct personal business on company time.	5	4	3	2	1
9. A manager may exaggerate a bit on quality or delivery date, if it means getting a big order.	1	2	3	4	5
10. It's acceptable to pad an expense report up to about 10%.	1	2	3	4	5
11. Management should be allowed to conceal minor product deficiencies from the public.	1	2	3	4	5
12. Employees should not take pencils, tools, etc. home for personal use.	5	4	3	2	1
13. Managers should not set unreasonable goals to push for better worker performance.	5	4	3	2	1
14. It's acceptable for a worker to work slower than he/she is capable of working.	1	2	3	4	5
15. A manager may tell a worker to violate rules to help the firm meet a shipping date.	1	2	3	4	5
16. There's no problem if an employee takes extra time for lunch or break time.	1	2	3	4	5
17. A manager should not violate a safety rule even if it means losing a big order.	5	4	3	2	1
18. WATS lines should never be used by employees for personal long-distance telephone calls.	5	4	3	2	1
19. Management should not divulge confidential information about an employee.	5	4	3	2	1
20. An employee should not accept gifts from salespersons in exchange for preferential treatment.	5	4	3	2	1

The Ethics Questionnaire Scoring Sheet

Transfer your numeric responses from the questionnaire onto this scoring sheet and sum the item to find your scores. Place an X on each of the continuums to indicate your scores.

Managerial Ethics		Employee Ethics	
Question No.	*Score*	*Question No.*	*Score*
1	_____	2	_____
3	_____	4	_____
5	_____	6	_____
7	_____	8	_____
9	_____	10	_____
11	_____	12	_____
13	_____	14	_____
15	_____	16	_____
17	_____	18	_____
19	_____	20	_____
Total:	_____	Total:	_____

Grand Total:_____

```
  |-----|-----|-----|-----|-----|
 50    40    30    20    10     0
```
The Managerial Ethics Continuum

```
  |-----|-----|-----|-----|-----|
 50    40    30    20    10     0
```
The Employee Ethics Continuum

```
  |----|----|----|----|----|----|----|----|----|----|
 100   90   80   70   60   50   40   30   20   10    0
```
The Ethics Continuum

42

CHAPTER 5 THE GLOBAL CONTEXT OF MANAGEMENT

Exercise 5.1—Planning the Overseas Venture

PURPOSE

Help students understand that business environmental factors differ significantly from one country to another

TIME REQUIRED

45 minutes

   Step 1: Small-group research activity (completed before class)

   Step 2: Class discussion (45 minutes)

MATERIALS NEEDED

None

PROCEDURE

Step 1: The instructor will divide the class into small groups and assign each group the task of researching the business environment and completing The Overseas Venture Planning Guide (pp. 45–46) for one of the following overseas business ventures:

  1. Selling an instant rice breakfast cereal in Japan
  2. Selling canned condensed soup in Guatemala
  3. Selling low calorie Jello in Taiwan
  4. Selling Walkman radios in Chad
  5. Selling men's cosmetics in China
  6. Manufacturing pocket calculators in Somalia

   Students may obtain the needed information through library research or by interviewing people with knowledge of the country and/or product in question.

Step 2: A representative(s) from each group will present the group's findings for class discussion.

The Overseas Venture Planning Guide

Overseas Venture Assigned:_____

For each international variable category, list (1) the different or difficult conditions that can be expected, and (2) the resultant implications for management.

International Variable	Different or Difficult Conditions to Expect	Implications for Management
Business Customs		
Cultural/Social		
Economic/Fiscal		
Family Adjustment		

International Variable	Different or Difficult Conditions to Expect	Implications for Management
Foreign Language		
Infrastructure		
Labor Factors		
Market Factors		
Political/Legal		

Exercise 5.2—Training U.S. Expatriates

PURPOSE

Help students develop an appreciation for the complexities involved in the training of U.S. personnel assigned to overseas positions

TIME REQUIRED

45 minutes

    Step 1: Individual activity (10 minutes)

    Step 2: Small-group activity (20 minutes)

    Step 3: Class discussion (15 minutes)

MATERIALS NEEDED

None

PROCEDURE

Step 1: Each student should read The U.S. Expatriate Training Problem and complete The U.S. Expatriate Training Survey (p. 49).

THE U.S. EXPATRIATE TRAINING PROBLEM

We all hear the stories about how U.S. firms and/or products often fail in a foreign environment because they seem to be insensitive to the uniqueness of foreign environments. For example, when Chevrolet introduced its new Nova, it didn't sell in Spanish-speaking countries where the name Nova means "It doesn't go." Not to be outdone, Ford also found poor sales for its Fiera truck in Spanish-speaking countries, where the name Fiera means "ugly old woman." Therefore, progressive U.S. firms are now devoting more attention to the selection and training of people to be given foreign assignments.

Step 2: The instructor will divide the class into small groups. Each group will achieve consensus on the rankings in the U.S. Expatriate Training Survey and develop group responses to the discussion questions.

Step 3: A representative from each group will present the group's findings for class discussion.

QUESTIONS FOR DISCUSSION

1. Why would foreign language training be of utmost importance to U.S. expatriates?
2. Why do many U.S. companies neither require nor provide foreign language training?
3. What kind of family adjustment problems might U.S. expatriates have in some countries?

The U.S. Expatriate Training Survey

Rank-order the relative importance of the following nine categories of training that might be provided to U.S. expatriates before they are given overseas assignments of (1) short-term duration (up to three months) or (2) long-term duration (one year or more). A rank of 1 should go to the most important training category and a rank of 9 to the least important category. In Step 2, you can add the group ranking. In Step 3, the instructor will give you the ranking by Fortune 500 firms.

Training Category	Short-Term Rank			Long-Term Rank		
	Your	*Group*	*500*	*Your*	*Group*	*500*
Business Customs	___	___	___	___	___	___
Cultural/Social Factors	___	___	___	___	___	___
Economic/Fiscal Factors	___	___	___	___	___	___
Family Adjustment	___	___	___	___	___	___
Foreign Language	___	___	___	___	___	___
Infrastructure	___	___	___	___	___	___
Market Factors	___	___	___	___	___	___
Labor Factors	___	___	___	___	___	___
Political/Legal Factors	___	___	___	___	___	___

Exercise 5.3—Overseas Management Issues

PURPOSE

Help students understand the issues of placing and keeping good managers in overseas positions

TIME REQUIRED

45 minutes

    Step 1: Individual activity (completed before class)

    Step 2: Small-group activity (30 minutes)

    Step 3: Class discussion (15 minutes)

MATERIALS NEEDED

None

PROCEDURE

Step 1: Before class, each student should: (1) read U.S. Expatriates' Placement Problems, (2) complete The Overseas Selection Criteria Survey (p. 53), and (3) complete The Overseas Abortment Survey (p. 55).

U.S. EXPATRIATES' PLACEMENT PROBLEMS

Somewhere between 20 and 40 percent of all U.S. overseas postings turn out to be mistakes for both the expatriate and the employing institution. The dollar costs of such mistakes can run into the millions or even result in the total collapse of the institution. Critics suggest that there are two basic reasons behind this exceptional failure rate. First, it would seem that employers do not use the proper criteria when selecting people for overseas postings. Second, it would seem that employers do not have an adequate understanding of why people abort their overseas postings before their assignments are adequately completed.

Step 2: The instructor will divide the class into small groups. Each group will achieve consensus on the rankings on the two surveys.

Step 3: A representative from each group will present the group's findings for class discussion.

The Overseas Selection Criteria Survey

You are to rank-order the following 12 selection criteria with respect to their relative importance in selecting a U.S. worker for an overseas assignment. A rank of 1 should be given to the most important criterion and a rank of 12 to the least important. In Step 2, you can record the group ranking. In Step 3, the instructor will give you the rankings of the Fortune 500 firms.

	Ranking		
Selection Criterion	*Your*	*Group*	*500*
Adaptability	———	———	———
Cultural Empathy	———	———	———
Diplomatic Skills	———	———	———
Emotional Stability	———	———	———
Family	———	———	———
Health/Age	———	———	———
Language Skills	———	———	———
Overseas Experience	———	———	———
Past Performance	———	———	———
Personal Motives	———	———	———
Personality	———	———	———
Technical Skills	———	———	———

The Overseas Abortment Survey

You are to rank-order the following nine reasons for U.S. expatriates' aborting their overseas assignments before they are adequately completed. A rank of 1 should be given to the most important reason and a rank of 9 to the least important reasons. In Step 2, you can record the group ranking. In Step 3, the instructor will give you the ranking by Fortune 500 firms.

	Ranking		
Abortment Reason	*Your*	*Group*	*500*
Blocked Promotions	————	————	————
Business Customs	————	————	————
Cultural/Social	————	————	————
Health/Personal	————	————	————
Income Gaps/Cost	————	————	————
Language	————	————	————
Leadership Style	————	————	————
Political/Legal	————	————	————
Religion	————	————	————

CHAPTER 6   MANAGING ORGANIZATIONAL GOALS AND PLANNING

Exercise 6.1—Developing Business Missions and Goals

PURPOSE

Help students develop the skills needed to develop mission statements and goal statements for businesses

TIME REQUIRED

45 minutes

Step 1: Individual activity (completed before class)

Step 2: Small-group activity (30 minutes)

Step 3: Class discussion (15 minutes)

MATERIALS NEEDED

None

PROCEDURE

Step 1:   Before class, each student should study (1) Table 6.1, Components of Corporate Mission Statements, (2) Figure 6.2, Kinds of Organizational Goals for a Regional Fast Food Chain, and (3) the text materials on mission and goal statements.

Step 2:   The instructor will divide the class into small groups, assigning each group one of the following organizations:

1. Regional department store chain
2. County hospital
3. Local health and fitness center
4. Resort hotel
5. Local bowling alley
6. Regional supermarket chain
7. Local beauty parlor
8. State university
9. Regional newspaper
10. Local insurance agency

Organization Assigned: _____

Using Table 6.1 and Figure 6.2 as guides, each group will complete The Mission Statement Worksheet (p. 61) and The Organizational Goals Worksheet for the assigned organization (p. 63).

Step 3:   One representative from each group should present the group's findings to the class.

TABLE 6.1

Components of Corporate Mission Statements

Target Customers and Markets

Example: "We believe our first responsibility is to the doctors, nurses, and patients, to mothers and all others who use our products." (Johnson & Johnson)

Principal Products or Services

Example: "AMAX's principal products are molybdenum, coal, iron ore, copper, lead, zinc, petroleum and natural gas, potash, phosphates, nickel, tungsten, silver, gold, and magnesium."

Geographic Domain

Example: "We are dedicated to the total success of Corning Glass Works as a worldwide competitor."

Core Technologies

Example: "Control Data is in the business of applying micro-electronics and computer technology in two general areas: computer-related hardware; and computing-enhancing services, which include computation, information, education, and finance."

Concern for Survival, Growth, and Profitability

Example: "In this respect, the company will conduct its operations prudently, and will provide the profits and growth which will assure Hoover's ultimate success." (Hoover Universal)

Company Philosophy

Example: "It's all part of the Mary Kay philosophy—a philosophy based on the golden rule. A spirit of sharing and caring where people give cheerfully of their time, knowledge, and experience." (Mary Kay Cosmetics)

Company Self-Concept

Example: "Hoover Universal is a diversified, multi-industry corporation with strong manufacturing capabilities, entrepreneurial policies, and individual business unit autonomy."

Desired Public Image

Example: "To share the world's obligation for the protection of the environment." (Dow Chemical)

From John A. Pearce II and Fred David, "Corporate Mission Statements: The Bottom Line," from Academy of Management *Executive,* May 1987, pp. 109–115. Reprinted by permission of the Academy of Management *Executive,* and the authors.

Mission: Our mission is to operate a chain of restaurants that will prepare and serve high-quality food on a timely basis and at reasonable prices.

Strategic goals

President and CEO

- Provide 14% return to investors for at least 10 years
- Start or purchase new restaurant chain within 5 years
- Negotiate new labor contract this year

Tactical goals

Vice president—operations

- Open 150 new restaurants during next 10 years
- Decrease food-container costs by 15% during next 5 years
- Decrease average customer wait by 30 seconds this year

Vice president—marketing

- Increase per store sales 5% per year for 10 years
- Target and attract 2 new market segments during next 5 years
- Develop new promotional strategy for next year

Vice president—finance

- Keep corporate debt to no more than 20% of liquid assets for next 10 years
- Develop computerized accounting system within 5 years
- Earn 9% on excess cash this year

Operational goals

Restaurant manager

- Implement employee incentive system within 2 years
- Decrease waste by 5% this year
- Hire and train new assistant manager

Advertising director

- Develop regional advertising campaigns within 3 years
- Negotiate 5% lower advertising rates next year
- Implement this year's promotional strategy

Accounting manager

- Split accounts receivable/payable functions from other areas within 2 years
- Computerize payroll system for each restaurant this year
- Pay all invoices within 30 days

FIGURE 6.2
Kinds of Organizational Goals for a Regional Fast Food Chain (Reprinted from Ricky Griffin, *Management,* 3rd ed., copyright © Houghton Mifflin Company 1990. Used by permission.)

The Mission Statement Worksheet for _____

Target Customers and Markets: _____

_____

_____

_____

Principal Products and Services: _____

_____

_____

_____

Geographic Domain: _____

_____

_____

_____

Core Technologies: _____

_____

_____

_____

Concern for Survival, Growth and Profitability: _____

_____

_____

_____

Company Philosophy: _____

_____

_____

_____

Company Self-Concept: _____

_____

_____

_____

Desired Public Image: _____

_____

_____

_____

Organizational Goals Worksheet for _____

Strategic goals

President/CEO

Tactical goals

VP—operations	VP—marketing	VP—finance

Operational goals

Operations manager	Advertising manager	Accounting manager

Exercise 6.2—Goal Setting

PURPOSE

Help students develop the skills needed for effective goal setting

TIME REQUIRED

45 minutes

   Step 1: Individual activity (5 minutes)
   Step 2: Small-group activity (25 minutes)
   Step 3: Class discussion (15 minutes)

MATERIALS NEEDED

None

PROCEDURE

Step 1:   Students should study the following guidelines for effective goal setting.

GUIDELINES FOR EFFECTIVE GOAL SETTING

1. *Action orientation*   Every goal statement should be described in terms of the action required to reach that goal. Therefore, each goal statement should (1) start with the word *to,* which should (2) be followed by an action verb (e.g., improve, achieve, increase, etc.).
2. *Results orientation*   Every goal statement should specify a single key result to be achieved (e.g., market standing, innovation, productivity, profitability, etc.).
3. *Measurability*   Every goal statement should specify a single key result that is objective and quantifiably measurable. That is, "To be a better manager" may sound like an admirable goal, but it is not objective and quantifiably measurable.
4. *Time certainty*   Every goal statement should specify a target date for goal achievement.

Step 2:   The instructor will divide the class into small groups. Each group shall apply the above guidelines for effective goal setting to the Goal-Setting Worksheet on pp. 67–68 and develop group responses to the discussion questions.

Step 3:   One representative from each group should present the group's findings and the group's responses to the discussion questions to the class.

QUESTIONS FOR DISCUSSION

1. What was the most difficult part of the assignment?
2. Why do you think people resist establishing goals in this manner?
3. Do you think you will now set goals for yourself in this manner?

Goal-Setting Worksheet

Write three performance goals for each of the following positions, using the guidelines for effective goal setting.

Position	Action Orientation	Results Orientation	Measurability	Time Certainty
Computer Repair Person	1. To			
	2. To			
	3. To			
College Student	1. To			
	2. To			
	3. To			
Hospital Nursing Supervisor	1. To			
	2. To			
	3. To			
Campus Security Officer	1. To			
	2. To			
	3. To			
Movie Theater Manager	1. To			
	2. To			
	3. To			
Certified Public Accountant	1. To			
	2. To			
	3. To			
Criminal Court Judge	1. To			
	2. To			
	3. To			
Savings And Loan CEO	1. To			
	2. To			
	3. To			

Position	Action Orientation	Results Orientation	Measurability	Time Certainty
Newspaper Reporter	1. To			
	2. To			
	3. To			

Exercise 6.3—Goal-Setting Questionnaire

PURPOSE

Help students understand the elements of goal setting and their own goal-setting tendencies

TIME REQUIRED

45 minutes

    Step 1: Individual activity (15 minutes)

    Step 2: Small-group activity (15 minutes)

    Step 3: Class discussion (15 minutes)

MATERIALS NEEDED

None

PROCEDURE

Step 1: Students should think back to the times when they have been required to set goals for them-selves and indicate their perception of their goal-setting behaviors and feelings by circling the appropriate number on the scale for each statement on the Goal-Setting Questionnaire (see p. 71). Then the instru-ment should be scored in accordance with the instructions on the scoring sheet on p. 72.

Step 2: The instructor will divide the class into small groups. Each group should compute the group's average score, analyze the differences in individual scores, and develop group responses to the discussion questions.

Step 3: The instructor may collect the group-average scores in order to compute the class average score. Group representatives can then make group reports and respond to the discussion questions.

QUESTIONS FOR DISCUSSION

1. What common patterns exist in questionnaire responses?
2. What might account for differences in individual responses?
3. What goal-setting patterns are best for the employing organization? For the individual?

Goal-Setting Questionnaire

Statement	Strongly Agree	Slightly Agree	Not Sure	Slightly Disagree	Strongly Disagree
1. Rewards should be allocated based on goal achievement.	5	4	3	2	1
2. I set goals for all key results areas.	5	4	3	2	1
3. Goals should have clear deadlines.	5	4	3	2	1
4. I work hard to give others feedback on how they're doing.	5	4	3	2	1
5. I tend to set goals that I can't quite achieve to force me to try harder.	1	2	3	4	5
6. Sometimes, when I think maybe I'm not doing so well, I don't want feedback from others.	1	2	3	4	5
7. My goals are always clearly stated.	1	2	3	4	5
8. My goals are stated in quantifiable terms.	5	4	3	2	1
9. Achieving goals is the way to promotion and success.	5	4	3	2	1
10. My boss (parent, etc.) will not get on my case if I don't achieve my goals.	1	2	3	4	5
11. My boss (parent, etc.) usually sets my goals.	1	2	3	4	5
12. I don't always know what the key results areas are.	1	2	3	4	5
13. I work better without specific deadlines.	1	2	3	4	5
14. Others allow me to take part in setting my goals.	5	4	3	2	1
15. The more challenging my goals, the better I work.	5	4	3	2	1
16. If I'm not on target to achieve my goals, my boss (parent, etc.) should get on my case.	5	4	3	2	1
17. When I'm working on my goals, my boss (parent, etc.) doesn't always give me the support I need.	1	2	3	4	5
18. Specific goals make me nervous, so I prefer general goals.	1	2	3	4	5
19. My goals state exactly what results I plan to achieve.	5	4	3	2	1
20. I challenge myself by setting goals that are just out of my reach.	1	2	3	4	5

Goal-Setting Questionnaire Scoring Sheet

Sum all of your responses on the questionnaire and place your total score here: _____

Group-average Score: _____

Class-average Score: _____

CHAPTER 7   MANAGING STRATEGY AND STRATEGIC PLANNING

Exercise 7.1—The SWOT Analysis

PURPOSE

Help students understand the complex interrelationships between environmental opportunities and threats and organizational strengths and weaknesses

TIME REQUIRED

45 minutes

> Step 1: Individual activity (5 minutes)
>
> Step 2: Small-group activity (25 minutes)
>
> Step 3: Class discussion (15 minutes)

MATERIALS NEEDED

None

PROCEDURE

Step 1: Each student should study Figure 7.2, Strategy Formulation at Marriott, and the text materials concerning the matching of organizations with environments.

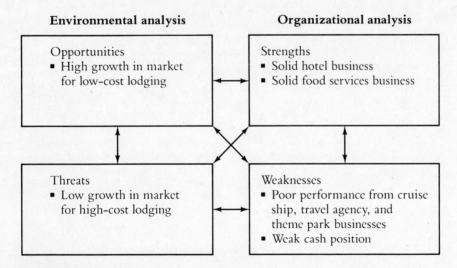

FIGURE 7.2
Strategy Formulation at Marriott (Reprinted from Ricky Griffin, *Management,* 3rd ed., p. 198. Copyright © Houghton Mifflin Company 1990. Used by permission.)

Step 2:   The instructor will divide the class into small groups. Each group will conduct a SWOT (strengths, weaknesses, opportunities, threats) Analysis for Marriott on pp. 75–76 and prepare group responses to the discussion questions. Marriott has been successful in its hotel and food services businesses but less than successful in its cruise ship, travel agency, and theme park businesses.

Strategy formulation is facilitated by a SWOT Analysis. First the organization should study its internal operations in order to identify its strengths and weaknesses. Next, the organization should scan the environment in order to identify existing and future opportunities and threats. Then the organization should identify the relationships that exist among the strengths, weaknesses, opportunities, and threats. Finally, major business strategies usually result from matching an organization's opportunities with appropriate opportunities or from matching threats with weaknesses. To facilitate the environmental analysis in search of opportunities and threats, it is helpful to break the environment down into its major components—international, economic, political-legal, sociocultural, and technological.

Step 3:   One representative from each group may be asked to report on the group's SWOT Analysis and to report the group's responses to the discussion questions.

QUESTIONS FOR DISCUSSION

1. What was the most difficult part of the SWOT Analysis?
2. Why do most firms not develop major strategies for matches between threats and strengths?
3. Under what conditions might a firm develop a major strategy around a match between an opportunity and a weakness?

Marriott SWOT Analysis Sheet

Environmental analysis   **Organizational analysis**

Opportunities
_____
_____
_____
_____
_____
_____
_____
_____
_____
_____
_____
_____
_____
_____

Strengths
_____
_____
_____
_____
_____
_____
_____
_____
_____
_____
_____
_____
_____
_____

Threats
_____
_____
_____
_____
_____
_____
_____
_____
_____
_____
_____
_____
_____

Weaknesses
_____
_____
_____
_____
_____
_____
_____
_____
_____
_____
_____
_____
_____
_____

Relationships Between Opportunities and Strengths

1. _____
2. _____
3. _____

Relationships Between Opportunities and Weaknesses

1. _____
2. _____
3. _____

Relationships Between Threats and Strengths

1. _____
2. _____
3. _____

Relationships Between Threats and Weaknesses

1. _____
2. _____
3. _____

Major Strategies Matching Opportunities with Strengths

1. _____
2. _____
3. _____
4. _____

Major Strategies Matching Threats with Weaknesses

1. _____
2. _____
3. _____
4. _____

Exercise 7.2—Using the BCG Matrix

PURPOSE

Help students understand how to use the Boston Consulting Group (BCG) portfolio matrix as a tool for formulating or evaluating corporate strategy

TIME REQUIRED

45 minutes

    Step 1: Group library activity (completed before class)

    Step 2: Small-group activity (30 minutes)

    Step 3: Class discussion (15 minutes)

MATERIALS NEEDED

None

PROCEDURE

Step 1: The instructor will divide the class into small groups and assign each group two (or more) corporate strategic business units (SBUs) to be researched in the library as needed to complete BCG analyses. Students will find the required information in the library business reference books, corporate annual reports, and key business periodicals. To complete this exercise effectively, students will probably find the following notes to be helpful.

STUDENT NOTES

1. Grand strategy is that overall corporate strategy that defines missions and strategic goals for the overall organization and guides the strategic management of all corporate entities. There are three types of grand strategies: (1) growth strategies, (2) retrenchment strategies, and (3) stability strategies.

2. The definition of a strategic business unit (SBU) may vary from firm to firm and from industry to industry. However, an SBU is normally defined as a separate division within the corporation that has its own mission and strategy.

3. The Boston Consulting Group (BCG) matrix was developed to analyze SBUs according to two criteria: (1) the annual growth rate of its market, and (2) its relative share of that market. As shown in The BCG Matrix Worksheet, the matrix categorizes each SBU as a Star, Cash Cow, Question Mark, or Dog. The Star has a relatively large share of a growing market. The Cash Cow has a relatively large share of a market without growth. The Question Mark has a relatively small share of a growing market. The Dog, sometimes called the Cash Trap, has a relatively small share of a market without growth.

    An SBU's relative market share is its share relative to the industry's top shareholder. For example, an SBU with 10 percent of a market led by a competitor that has 35 percent of the market has a relative market share of $.10/.35 = 0.29$. The BCG Matrix dividing line that separates Stars from

Cash Cows is 10 percent. The dividing line that separates Stars from Question Marks is 1.0. The SBU is placed in its appropriate position on the matrix in the form of a circle, the size of which is proportional to the amount of revenues contributed by that SBU to the corporation (the larger the circle, the greater the contribution).

Step 2:   The instructor will ask each group to meet and complete the following tasks:

1. Place the SBUs on the BCG Matrix Worksheet on p. 79.
2. Develop a grand strategy for each SBU on p. 81.

Step 3:   One representative from each group will report the group's decisions.

BCG Matrix Worksheet

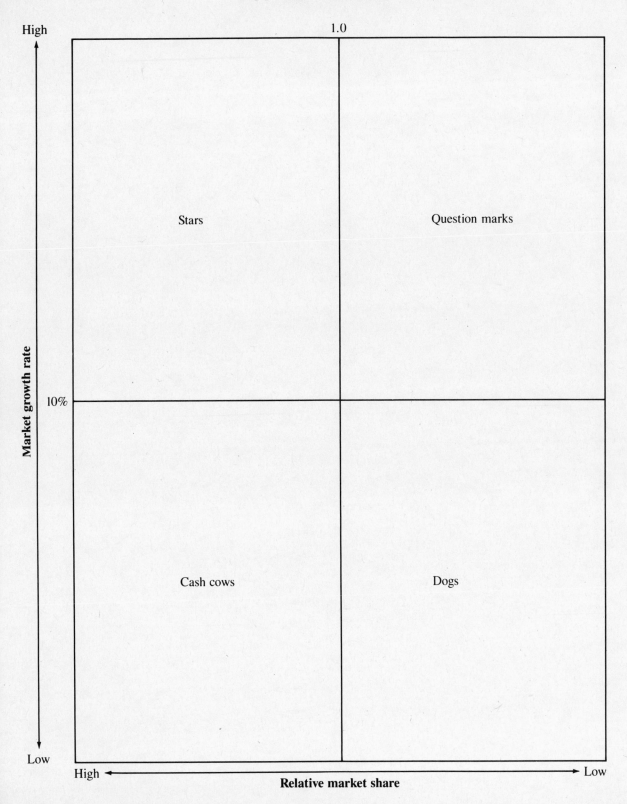

High   1.0

Market growth rate

Stars

Question marks

10%

Cash cows

Dogs

Low

High ⟵   **Relative market share**   ⟶ Low

Ricky Griffin, *Management,* 3rd ed., p. 202. Copyright © Houghton Mifflin Company 1990. Used by permission. Originally adapted from the Product Portfolio Matrix, 1970, The Boston Consulting Group, Inc.

SBU Grand Strategy Worksheet

SBU Assigned	BCG Category	Strategy Category	Strategy Description
_____	_____	_____	_____
_____	_____	_____	_____
_____	_____	_____	_____
_____	_____	_____	_____
_____	_____	_____	_____
_____	_____	_____	_____

Exercise 7.3—Developing Functional Strategies

PURPOSE

Help students understand the nature and relationships of corporate functional strategies

TIME REQUIRED

45 minutes

  Step 1: Group library activity (completed before class)
  Step 2: Small-group activity (30 minutes)
  Step 3: Class discussion (15 minutes)

MATERIALS NEEDED

None

PROCEDURE

Step 1: The instructor will divide the class into small groups and assign each group a corporation to be researched in the library for the purpose of completing the sections on marketing, finance, production, research and development, and human resource management as shown on the Functional Strategies Worksheet on pp. 85–86. Students will find the required information about the assigned corporation in the library business reference books, corporate annual reports, and key business periodicals.

Step 2: The instructor will ask each group to complete the Functional Strategies Worksheet by developing one strategy for each of the 18 functional concerns.

Step 3: One representative from each group will present the group's strategies.

Functional Strategies Worksheet

Corporation Assigned: _____

Functional Area	Major Concerns	Strategy Description
Marketing	1. Product Mix	_____
		_____
	2. Market Position	_____
		_____
	3. Distribution	_____
		_____
	4. Sales Promotions	_____
		_____
	5. Pricing	_____
		_____
	6. Public Policy	_____
		_____
Finance	7. Debt Policy	_____
		_____
	8. Dividend Policy	_____
		_____
Production	9. Productivity	_____
		_____
	10. Production Planning	_____
		_____
	11. Plant Location	_____
		_____
	12. Government Regulation	_____
		_____
Research and Development	13. Product Development	_____
		_____
	14. Technological Forecasting	_____
		_____
Human Resource Management	15. Personnel Policies	_____
		_____
	16. Labor Relations	_____
		_____

Functional Area	Major Concerns	Strategy Description
	17. Executive Development	_____ _____
	18. Government Regulation	_____ _____

CHAPTER 8   MANAGERIAL DECISION MAKING

Exercise 8.1—Discussion Methods and Problem Solving[1]

PURPOSE

Help students understand that individuals are better than groups at solving some problems, while groups are better than individuals at solving other problems

TIME REQUIRED

45 minutes

    Step 1: Small-group activity (30 minutes)

    Step 2: Class discussion (15 minutes)

MATERIALS NEEDED

None

PROCEDURE

Step 1:   The instructor will divide the class into small groups. Each group will solve the following four problems, within the required time limitations.

Problem 1:   (Allow only 3 minutes) Make up as many words as possible from the letters in the word *industrial.*

Problem 2:   (Allow only 5 minutes) Pass through all nine dots with only four straight lines, without raising your pencil from the papers. Retracing is not permitted, but a dot may be passed through by more than one line.

Problem 3:   (Allow only 5 minutes) If a chicken and a half can lay an egg and a half in a day and a half, how long will it take six chickens to lay twelve eggs?

---

1. Problems 1–4 are adapted from Norman R. F. Maier, *Psychology in Industrial Organizations,* 4th ed. (Boston: Houghton Mifflin, 1973), pp. 326–328. Used by permission.

Problem 4:   (Allow only 15 minutes) A supervisor has an extra sum of money in his budget for pay increases. He could distribute this money by: (a) giving all employees equal lump sums, (b) giving each worker an equal percentage increase in pay, (c) giving increments recognizing differences in need (e.g., dependents, illness in family), (d) giving higher increases to the better workers, and (e) giving increases relative to length of service. The assignment for each group is to reach a decision on the weight (expressed in percent) to give each criterion. All the extra money is to be allocated.

Step 2:   One representative from each group should present the group's decisions and their responses to the discussion questions.

QUESTIONS FOR DISCUSSION

1. For which of the problems was group discussion most helpful?
2. For which problems was group discussion least helpful?
3. Are groups better than individuals at solving some problems?
4. Are individuals better than groups at solving some problems?

Exercise 8.2—Problem-Solving Style Questionnaire (PSSQ)

PURPOSE

Help students understand the nature of problem-solving approaches as well as their own problem-solving styles

TIME REQUIRED

45 minutes

 Step 1: Individual activity (completed before class)
 Step 2: Minilecture on problem-solving styles (10 minutes)
 Step 3: Small-group activity (20 minutes)
 Step 4: Class discussion (15 minutes)

MATERIALS NEEDED

None

PROCEDURE

Step 1: This questionnaire is designed to measure the student's problem-solving style. Students should think back to situations in which they have had to make decisions, and they should respond to each statement on p. 91 by circling the appropriate number on the scale. Then they should score the instrument following the instructions on the scoring sheet, on p. 92.

Step 2: The instructor will give a minilecture explaining the nature of the four basic problem-solving styles: (1) sensing types, (2) intuitive types, (3) thinking types, and (4) feeling types.

Step 3: The instructor will divide the class into small groups. Each group should compute its average scores for the four types, analyze the differences in individual scores, and develop group responses to the discussion questions.

Step 4: The instructor may collect the groups' average scores in order to compute class-average scores. Group representatives can then respond to the discussion questions.

QUESTIONS FOR DISCUSSION

1. For which types are the scores more in agreement? Less in agreement?
2. What might account for the differences in individual scores?
3. How can the results of this test be put to constructive use?

Problem-Solving Style Questionnaire (PSSQ)

Statement	Strongly Agree	Slightly Agree	Not Sure	Slightly Disagree	Strongly Disagree
1. Most people think that I am objective and logical.	5	4	3	2	1
2. Most people would say that I am emotional and rather motivating.	5	4	3	2	1
3. Most people believe that I know the details of my job and do it very accurately.	5	4	3	2	1
4. Most people agree that I am a complex and intellectual person.	5	4	3	2	1
5. I tend to focus on immediate problems and let others worry about the distant future.	5	4	3	2	1
6. I try to please others and need occasional praise myself.	5	4	3	2	1
7. When I face a problem, I try to analyze all the facts and put them in systematic order.	5	4	3	2	1
8. I'm more interested in long-range implications and am often bored with minor here and now details.	5	4	3	2	1
9. I'm usually more people oriented than task oriented.	5	4	3	2	1
10. Before I put energy into a project, I want to know what's in it for me.	5	4	3	2	1
11. I normally solve problems quickly without wasting a lot of time on details.	5	4	3	2	1
12. When I have a job to do, I do it, even if others' feelings might get hurt in the process.	5	4	3	2	1
13. I get bored with routine and prefer to deal with new and complicated challenges.	5	4	3	2	1
14. I'm a pretty good judge as to how others feel about problems.	5	4	3	2	1
15. I don't let problems upset me, no matter how difficult they are.	5	4	3	2	1
16. I like to do things that I do well, but I'm not comfortable trying to learn new skills.	5	4	3	2	1
17. I prefer harmony in a work group— otherwise efficiency suffers.	5	4	3	2	1
18. I really enjoy solving new problems.	5	4	3	2	1
19. I am a quick learner, but I don't like theoretical, futuristic concepts.	5	4	3	2	1
20. When necessary, I have no trouble making tough, hard-nosed decisions.	5	4	3	2	1

Problem-Solving Style Questionnaire Scoring Sheet

Transfer your numeric responses from the questionnaire onto this scoring sheet and sum the items to find your scores. For example, your sensing type score is the sum of your responses to statements 3, 5, 10, 16, and 19.

Sensing	Intuitive	Feeling	Thinking
3_____	4_____	2_____	1_____
5_____	8_____	6_____	7_____
10_____	11_____	9_____	12_____
16_____	13_____	14_____	15_____
19_____	18_____	17_____	20_____

Totals: _____ _____ _____ _____

CHAPTER 9   MANAGEMENT TOOLS FOR PLANNING AND DECISION MAKING

Exercise 9.1—Using Time-Series Information

PURPOSE

Help students understand the application of time-series analysis

TIME REQUIRED

45 minutes

Step 1: Individual activity (completed before class)

Step 2: Small-group activity (35 minutes)

Step 3: Class discussion (10 minutes)

MATERIALS NEEDED

None

PROCEDURE

Step 1:   Before class, each student should study The Time-Series Analysis Instruction.

TIME-SERIES ANALYSIS INSTRUCTION

Time-series analysis is a tool for using information about the past to predict the future. The variable to be studied (sales, for instance) is plotted against time, using a "best-fit" line to see if there is any meaningful trend line that can help predict future sales.

For example, suppose sales (in $ millions) for the XYZ Company over the past five years are as follows:

Year	Sales
1984	2.5
1985	3.0
1986	3.5
1987	4.0
1988	4.5

The first step is to plot the sales for the five-year period on a scattergram to see if there is a good trend line. If there is a good fit (good trend line), regression analysis can be used to calculate future sales.

SCATTERGRAM FOR XYZ COMPANY SALES

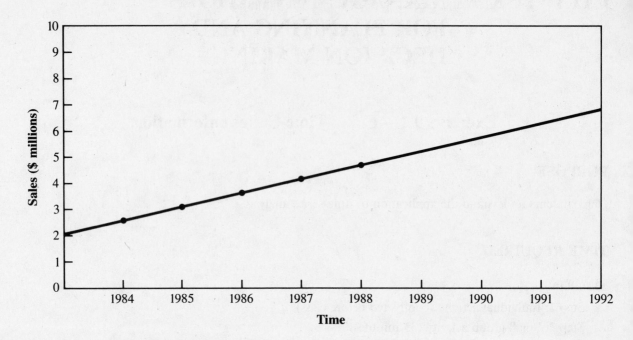

The XYZ Company scattergram shows a trend line with a good fit. The next step is to use regression analysis to estimate future sales. The line drawn in the scattergram is called a Regression Line because it shows the correlation (fit) between a dependent variable (sales) and an independent variable (time). The Regression Line is expressed mathematically by the Regression Equation, as follows:

Regression Equation:

$$y = a + bx$$

where: y = a dependent variable (sales)
x = an independent variable (time)
a = intercept point on the y axis
b = slope of the line (or the change in y per a change in x)

Slope is the amount by which y (sales) changes for each unit of increase in x (time)

Regression calculation: to calculate sales for the next four years.

$$y = a + bx \qquad a = y - bx \qquad b = \frac{\Sigma xy - N\bar{x}\bar{y}}{\Sigma x^2 - N\bar{x}^2}$$

Year	x	y	xy	x^2
1984	1	2.5	2.5	1
1985	2	3.0	6.0	4
1986	3	3.5	10.5	9
1987	4	4.0	16.0	16
1988	5	4.5	22.5	25
Totals:	15	17.5	57.5	55

$$\bar{x} = x/n = 15/5 = 3$$
$$\bar{y} = y/n = 17.5/5 = 3.5$$
$$N = 5$$

$$b = \frac{\Sigma xy - N\bar{x}\bar{y}}{\Sigma x^2 - N\bar{x}^2} = \frac{57.5 - (5)(3)(3.5)}{55 - (5)(9)} = .5$$

$$a = y - bx = 3.5 - (.5)(3) = 2$$

1989 sales $= y = a + bx = 2 + (.5)(6) = 5.0$
1990 sales $= y = a + bx = 2 + (.5)(7) = 5.5$
1991 sales $= y = a + bx = 2 + (.5)(8) = 6.0$
1992 sales $= y = a + bx = 2 + (.5)(9) = 6.5$

If you plot the sales for the years 1989–1992, you will see that they also fit along the regression line.

Step 2: The instructor will divide the class into small groups. Each group will solve the problem presented in The Importer's Dilemma (pp. 97–98).

Step 3: A representative from each group will present the group's findings for class discussion.

The Importer's Dilemma

An importer of Italian shoes has been importing Italian shoes for 10 years and wants an estimate of those imports for the next 4 years. The imports (in $ millions) have been as follows:

Year	Time Period x	y	xy	x^2
1979	1	1.5		
1980	2	1.8		
1981	3	2.0		
1982	4	2.4		
1983	5	2.8		
1984	6	3.0		
1985	7	3.3		
1986	8	3.5		
1987	9	3.9		
1988	10	4.2		
Totals	55	28.4		

Plot the 10 years' import data on the scattergram on the back of this worksheet. If there is a good fit, calculate the rest of the data in the chart above, calculate the imports for the next four years, and plot them on the scattergram.

Scattergram for Importer

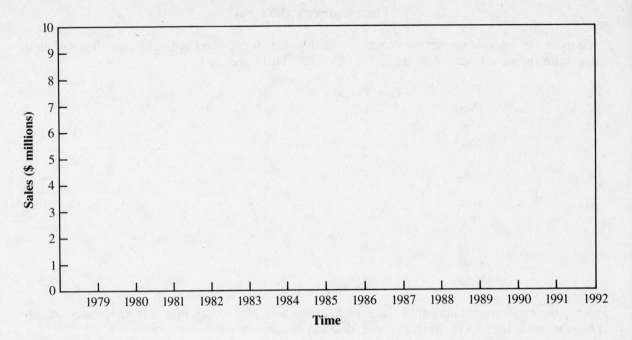

$N = 10$
$\bar{x} =$
$\bar{y} =$
$b =$
$a =$

1989 Sales $= y =$
1990 Sales $= y =$
1991 Sales $= y =$
1992 Sales $= y =$

98

Exercise 9.2—The Pert Network

PURPOSE

Help students understand the use of PERT networks and the critical path method for scheduling and managing complex operations

TIME REQUIRED

45 minutes

Step 1: Individual activity (completed before class)

Step 2: Small-group activity (30 minutes)

Step 3: Class discussion (15 minutes)

MATERIALS NEEDED

None

PROCEDURE

Step 1: Before class, each student should study A PERT Review.

A PERT REVIEW

PERT is an acronym for Program Evaluation and Review Technique. PERT is a graphic sequencing technique for scheduling and managing complex operations. In order to use PERT, the following terminology must be understood:

1. A PERT Event is a performance milestone that represents the start or completion of a PERT Activity.

2. A PERT Activity is time-consuming work that begins and ends with a PERT Event.

3. A PERT Network consists of the sequential PERT Events and PERT Activities required to complete a project. In a PERT Network, PERT Events are identified by letters of the alphabet and represented by circles connected by lines representing PERT Activities. The length of an activity line is not indicative of the time required to complete the activity. PERT Activities are represented by numbers. Thus, a simple PERT Network would be as follows:

$$\text{(A)} \overset{1}{\rule{2cm}{0.4pt}} \text{(B)} \overset{2}{\rule{2cm}{0.4pt}} \text{(C)}$$

4. A PERT Time is an estimated time for the completion of a PERT Activity. An Estimated PERT Time $[T_e]$ is the weighted average of three other time estimates: (1) Optimistic Time $[T_o]$, or the time the activity would take under ideal conditions; (2) Pessimistic Time $[T_p]$, or the time the activity would take under the worst conditions; and (3) Most Likely Time $[T_m]$, or the time the activity would take under normal conditions. The Estimated PERT Time $[T_e]$ is calculated as follows:

$$T_e = \frac{T_o + 4T_m + T_p}{6}$$

5. The Critical Path is the most time-consuming sequence of PERT activities and events in the PERT Network. It is the path that demands "Management by exception."

Step 2:   The instructor will divide the class into small groups. Each group will: (1) study The PERT Network Problem that follows, (2) construct a PERT Network (p. 103), (3) construct a Gantt chart (p. 105), and (4) develop a group response to the discussion questions.

THE PERT NETWORK PROBLEM

You are the members of a project team that has designed a new pull-toy product for children. You have been assigned the task of developing a PERT Network and a Gantt chart for the development and production of the first batch of the new pull-toy.

First, the team identified nine PERT Events, as follows:

A.   Top Management Approval to Begin

B.   Blueprints and Specifications Released

C.   Marketing Plan Completed

D.   Manufacturing Plan Completed

E.   Purchase Orders for Material Issued

F.   Financial Plan Completed

G.   Manufacturing Started

H.   Manufacturing Completed

I.   Pull-Toys Shipped

Second, the team identified ten major PERT activities for the project and collected the time estimates [T_o, T_m, T_p] for each activity. For each PERT Activity, the team identified a starting and an ending event.

	Events		Times			
PERT Activities	*Start*	*End*	T_o	T_p	T_m	T_e
1. Release Blueprints	A	B	3	1	2	
2. Develop Marketing Plan	A	C	2	5	4	
3. Develop Manufacturing Plan	B	D	3	6	5	
4. Develop Marketing Budget	C	F	3	8	6	
5. Develop Manufacturing Budget	D	F	4	7	5	
6. Prepare Manufacturing Orders	F	G	3	6	4	
7. Prepare Purchase Orders For Material	C	E	2	5	3	
8. Receive Material	E	G	7	11	9	
9. Manufacture Pull-Toys	G	H	8	13	10	
10. Test, Package, and Ship	H	I	3	6	4	

Step 3:   A representative of each group will present the group's findings for class discussion.

QUESTIONS FOR DISCUSSION

1. During the pull-toy project, the Marketing Manager notifies you that there will be a two-day delay in developing the marketing budget (Activity 4) unless overtime is authorized. Would you approve the overtime? Why or why not?

2. During the pull-toy project, the Manufacturing Manager notifies you that there will be a two-day delay in developing the manufacturing budget (Activity 5) unless overtime is authorized. Would you approve the overtime? Why or why not?

The Pull-Toy PERT Network

Using the information in the PERT Network Problem on p. 100, construct the PERT Network for the Pull-Toy Project. Identify the various paths through the network, calculating the Expected Time $[T_e]$ for each path, and identify the Critical Path for the project.

High-Path Events Sequence: A—
Middle-Path Events Sequence: A—
Low-Path Events Sequence: A—

The Pull-Toy Gantt Chart

Complete the Gantt Chart using the symbol ⌐‾‾‾⌐ to represent the Expected Time [T_e] scheduled for each activity.

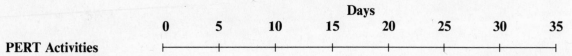

Days

| | 0 | 5 | 10 | 15 | 20 | 25 | 30 | 35 |

PERT Activities

1. Release Blueprints
2. Develop Marketing Plan
3. Develop Manufacturing Plan
4. Develop Marketing Budget
5. Develop Manufacturing Budget
6. Prepare Manufacturing Orders
7. Prepare Purchase Orders
8. Receive Material
9. Manufacture Pull-Toys
10. Test, Package, and Ship

Exercise 9.3—Using the Decision Tree and the Payoff Matrix

PURPOSE

Give students the opportunity to use two important decision-making tools (the decision tree and the payoff matrix) to facilitate a typical managerial decision

TIME REQUIRED

45 minutes

Step 1: Individual activity (5 minutes)

Step 2: Small-group activity (25 minutes)

Step 3: Class discussion (15 minutes)

MATERIALS NEEDED

None

PROCEDURE

Step 1: Each student should review the text materials on the use of decision trees and payoff matrices. Each student should then read The Problem Situation, which follows.

THE PROBLEM SITUATION

The Toyjoy Company has enjoyed three consecutive years of increased sales, but further growth will be possible only through major changes in production operations. The chief engineer has developed two growth plans. One plan is labor intensive and requires the hiring of more people and the use of overtime. The other plan is equipment intensive and involves considerable automation. The vice president of marketing is not sure about the sales forecast for the coming year and has placed a probability of 0.7 that sales will rise and a 0.3 probability that sales will decline. Using the cost figures provided by the chief engineer for the two different expansion plans and the sales probabilities provided by the vice president of marketing, the controller has calculated that by using the labor-intensive plan, the company's annual profit would be $500,000 if sales go up and $200,000 if sales go down. On the other hand, with the equipment-intensive plan, the firm's profits will be $485,000 if sales go up and $225,000 if sales go down. There is a staff meeting the following Tuesday to determine which plan to adopt.

Step 2: The instructor will divide the class into small groups. Each group is to complete The Decision Tree and The Payoff Matrix (see pp. 109–111), decide which plan to recommend, and develop group responses to the discussion questions.

Step 3: One representative from each group should present the group's findings, recommendations, and responses to the discussion questions.

QUESTIONS FOR DISCUSSION

1. Which expansion plan do you recommend? Why?

2. Even though one plan may provide greater profit potential, is that plan necessarily the best one for the company? Why?

3. What did you learn about quantitative decision-making tools from this exercise?

The Decision Tree

Decision/alternatives　　　　　**Events and probabilities**　　　　　**Expected payoffs**

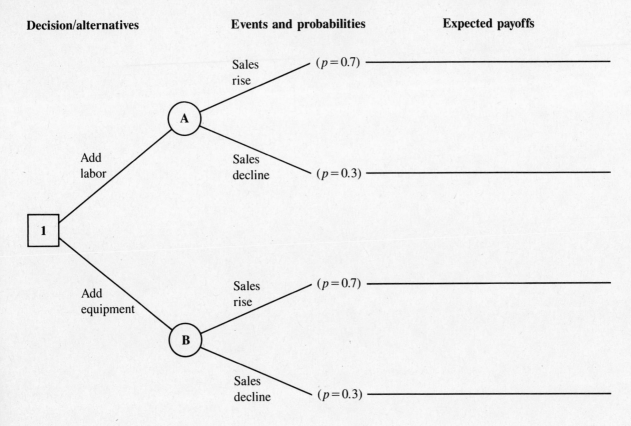

The Payoff Matrix

Possible Future Outcomes	Expected Value of Decision Alternatives	
	Add Labor	**Add Equipment**
Sales Rise	$EV = (p \times \$$_____)	$EV = (p \times \$$_____)
($p = 0.7$)	$EV = \$$_____	$EV = \$$_____
Sales Fall	$EV = (p \times \$$_____)	$EV = (p \times \$$_____)
($p = 0.3$)	$EV = \$$_____	$EV = \$$_____
Total EV	$EV = \$$_____	$EV = \$$_____

p = Probability
EV = Expected Value

CHAPTER 10   COMPONENTS OF ORGANIZATION STRUCTURE

Exercise 10.1—Organizing the School of Business

PURPOSE

Help students learn how to apply organization principles to the design of an organization

TIME REQUIRED

45 minutes

Step 1: Individual activity (10 minutes)

Step 2: Small-group activity (20 minutes)

Step 3: Class discussion (15 minutes)

MATERIALS NEEDED

None

PROCEDURE

Step 1:   Each student should study The School of Business Problem Situation.

THE SCHOOL OF BUSINESS PROBLEM SITUATION

You are a member of the Valley University School of Business Student Council. The new dean of the school has asked the Student Council to offer suggestions on ways the school can be organized to provide optimum service to all concerned. Valley University is a tax-supported institution, and its Business School serves 4,000 undergraduate business students and 300 MBA students in an urban area of 500,000 people. The dean's funding for staff has been authorized as follows:

- (1) Dean's Position plus the following:
  - (1) Secretary
  - (1) Administrative Assistant
  - (1) Development Officer (Fundraiser)
- (2) Associate Dean Positions
- (1) Graduate Director Position
- (1) Student Advising Supervisor and (3) Student Advisors
- (141) Teaching Faculty Positions, as follows:
  - (15) Accounting Faculty
  - (10) Economics Faculty
  - (18) Finance Faculty

        (8) International Business Faculty
      (25) Management Faculty
      (20) Management Information Systems Faculty
      (20) Marketing Faculty
      (25) Quantitative Studies Faculty
   (8) Department Chair Positions
   (1) Research Bureau Director Position responsible for:
      (1) Research Director and (2) Assistants
      (1) Grants Director and (2) Assistants
      (1) Journal Editor and (2) Assistants
      (1) Small-Business Institute Director
   (1) Continuing Education Director Position responsible for:
      (1) Management Development Center Director
         and (3) Assistants
      (1) Cooperative Education and Internships Director
         and (2) Assistants
   (1) Facilities Director Position responsible for:
      (1) Equipment Coordinator
      (1) Lab Coordinator
      (1) Word Processing Center Coordinator
         and (6) Assistants
(14) Secretaries

Furthermore, the School has a Business Advisory Council, composed of local community leaders, whose role is to give advice and counsel to the Dean. There is also the Business Associates group, composed of those people who contribute large amounts of money, equipment, and service to the School. Finally, there is the Student Council, which is composed of the officers of the business student organizations. The Student Council was formed to serve as a communication link between the School of Business and its students.

Using the above information, create the optimum organization chart for the Valley University Business School on page 115.

Step 2:   The instructor will divide the class into small groups. Each group is to develop an organization chart for The Valley University School of Business (p. 116) based on the information contained in The School of Business Problem Situation.

Step 3:   One representative from each group will present the group's decisions to the class.

QUESTIONS FOR DISCUSSION

1. What type(s) of departmentalization did most groups use?
2. What are the advantages and disadvantages of the types of departmentalization used?
3. Do you believe the span of control is appropriate in all areas?

The Valley University School of Business Organization Chart

The Valley University School of Business Organization Chart
(to be used by the group in step 2)

Exercise 10.2—Analyzing the Organization Chart

PURPOSE

Help students understand those organizational relationships that are represented by key characteristics found in organization charts

TIME REQUIRED

45 minutes

    Step 1: Individual activity (completed before class)

    Step 2: Small-group activity (30 minutes)

    Step 3: Class discussion (15 minutes)

MATERIALS NEEDED

None

PROCEDURE

Step 1:   Before class, each student should review the text materials with respect to critical organizational concepts, such as span of control, unity of command, chain of command, and line and staff.

Step 2:   The instructor will divide the class into small groups. Each group will study the organization chart for The Chaos Corporation on p. 118 and complete The Chaos Corporation Problem Worksheet on pp. 119–120. Each group should also be assigned the task of restructuring a portion of the organization (p. 121). For example, separate assignments could be made to reorganize the following elements of The Chaos Corporation:

    The Vice President's Staff Function

    The Personnel Function

    The Marketing Function

    The Finance Function

    The Production Function

    The Quality Assurance Function

    The Engineering Function

Step 3:   Group representatives will present the group's reports on the organization problems at The Chaos Corporation and the suggestions for corrective action.

The Chaos Corporation

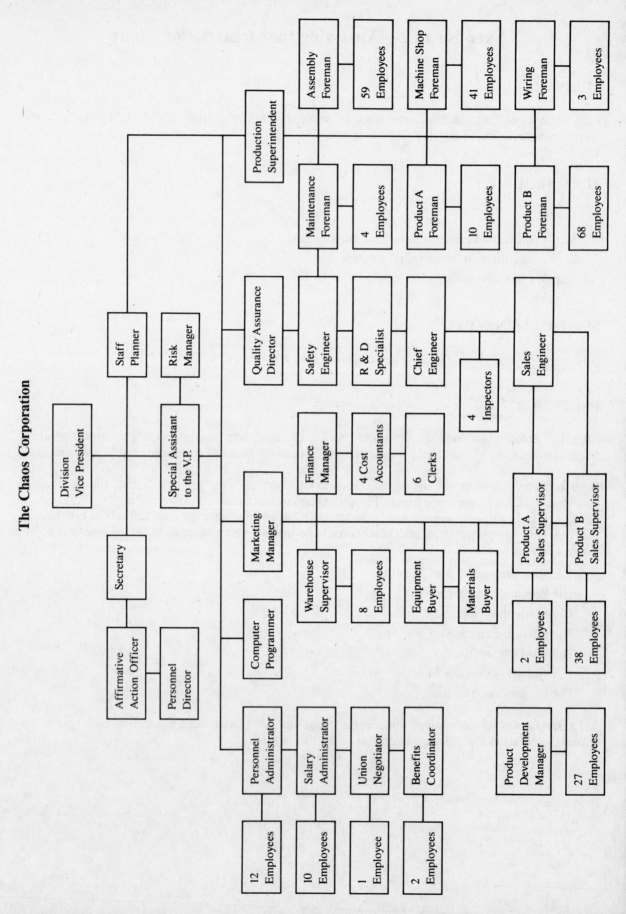

_____
Student's Name

Chaos Corporation Problem Worksheet

Problem Description   **Management Principle Involved**

1. _____   _____
   _____   _____
2. _____   _____
   _____   _____
3. _____   _____
   _____   _____
4. _____   _____
   _____   _____
5. _____   _____
   _____   _____
6. _____   _____
   _____   _____
7. _____   _____
   _____   _____
8. _____   _____
   _____   _____
9. _____   _____
   _____   _____
10. _____   _____
    _____   _____
11. _____   _____
    _____   _____
12. _____   _____
    _____   _____
13. _____   _____
    _____   _____
14. _____   _____
    _____   _____
15. _____   _____
    _____   _____
16. _____   _____
    _____   _____

Problem Description	Management Principle Involved
17. _____	_____
_____	_____
18. _____	_____
_____	_____
19. _____	_____
_____	_____
20. _____	_____
_____	_____

Student's Name

Proposed Reorganization of _____ **Function**

(Use the space below to show the reorganization proposal.)

Exercise 10.3—Delegation Aptitude Survey

PURPOSE

Help students gain an insight into the process of and the attitudes important to delegation

TIME REQUIRED

45 minutes

Step 1: Individual activity (15 minutes)
Step 2: Small-group activity (15 minutes)
Step 3: Class discussion (15 minutes)

MATERIALS NEEDED

None

PROCEDURE

Step 1: Each student should complete and score the Delegation Aptitude Survey on pp. 125–126. Students should think back to work or group situations in which they have had the opportunity to delegate responsibility to others. If they have not had such experiences, they should try to imagine how they would respond in such a situation. Then they should respond to each statement by circling the response that best typifies their attitude or behavior.

Step 2: The instructor will divide the class into small groups. Each group should compare scores, calculate a group-average score, and prepare group responses to the discussion questions.

Step 3: The instructor will collect group-average scores and calculate a class-average score. Then a representative from each group will present group responses to the discussion questions.

QUESTIONS FOR DISCUSSION

1. In what respects do the survey responses agree or disagree?
2. What might account for some of the differences in individual scores?
3. How can you make constructive use of the survey results?

Delegation Aptitude Survey

Statement	Strongly Agree	Slightly Agree	Not Sure	Slightly Disagree	Strongly Disagree
1. I don't think others can do the work as well as I can.	1	2	3	4	5
2. I often take work home with me.	1	2	3	4	5
3. Employees who can make their own decisions tend to be more efficient.	5	4	3	2	1
4. I often have to rush to meet deadlines.	1	2	3	4	5
5. Employees with more responsibility tend to have more commitment to group goals.	5	4	3	2	1
6. When I delegate, I always explain precisely how the task is to be done.	1	2	3	4	5
7. I always seem to have too much to do and too little time to do it in.	1	2	3	4	5
8. When employees have the responsibility to do a job, they usually do it well.	5	4	3	2	1
9. When I delegate, I make clear the end results I expect.	5	4	3	2	1
10. I usually only delegate simple, routine tasks.	1	2	3	4	5
11. When I delegate, I always make sure everyone concerned is so informed.	5	4	3	2	1
12. If I delegate, I usually wind up doing the job over again to get it right.	1	2	3	4	5
13. I become irritated watching others doing a job I can do better.	1	2	3	4	5
14. When I delegate, I feel I am losing the control I need.	1	2	3	4	5
15. When I delegate, I always set specific dates for progress reports.	5	4	3	2	1
16. When I do a job, I do it to perfection.	1	2	3	4	5
17. I honestly feel that I can do most jobs better than my subordinates can.	1	2	3	4	5
18. When employees make their own decisions, it tends to cause confusion.	1	2	3	4	5
19. It's difficult for subordinates to make decisions because they don't know the organization's goals.	1	2	3	4	5
20. When employees are given responsibility, they usually do what is asked of them.	5	4	3	2	1

Scoring Instructions

Calculate the sum of your responses to the 20 statements:

Your score _____

    This score represents your delegation aptitude. A maximum score would be 100, and a minimum score would be 20.

Mark your score with an X on the Delegation Aptitude Continuum.

100	90	80	70	60	50	40	30	20

The Delegation Aptitude Continuum

126

CHAPTER 11   MANAGING ORGANIZATION DESIGN

Exercise 11.1—The Mechanistic/Organic Organization Survey

PURPOSE

Help students understand the unique differences between mechanistic organizations and organic organizations

TIME REQUIRED

45 minutes

> Step 1: Individual activity (15 minutes)
> Step 2: Small-group activity (15 minutes)
> Step 3: Class discussion (15 minutes)

MATERIALS NEEDED

None

PROCEDURE

Step 1: Each student should complete and score the Mechanistic/Organic Organization Survey on pp. 129–130. Students should think back to work or other organizational experiences and respond to each statement by circling the response that best fits their impression of the organization. If they have no such experience to draw on, they should respond to the statements by identifying the organizational characteristics they would prefer.

Step 2: The instructor will divide the class into small groups. Each group should calculate its average mechanistic and organic scores. Using Interpreting the Mechanistic/Organic Organization Survey Scores on p. 131 as a guide, the group should discuss the interpretation of the scores. Then the students should develop responses to the discussion questions.

Step 3: A representative from each group will present group-average scores and the group's responses to the discussion questions.

QUESTIONS FOR DISCUSSION

1. Describe a mechanistic organization with which you are familiar. Describe an organic organization with which you are familiar.
2. If you were a subordinate, would you prefer to work in a mechanistic organization or an organic organization? Would your preference change if you were a manager?
3. Do you expect to work in a mechanistic or an organic environment?

Mechanistic/Organic Organization Survey

Statement	Strongly Agree	Slightly Agree	Not Sure	Slightly Disagree	Strongly Disagree
1. Jobs are clearly and precisely defined.	5	4	3	2	1
2. Rules are flexible enough to cope with exceptional cases.	1	2	3	4	5
3. Positions are arrayed in a clear and orderly hierarchy.	5	4	3	2	1
4. The organization is dedicated to the idea that each worker should be encouraged to fully develop his/her skills and abilities.	1	2	3	4	5
5. Rules and regulations are clear and are followed by everyone.	5	4	3	2	1
6. Only critical decisions must be approved by top management.	1	2	3	4	5
7. Most communications from above deal with instructions on how to do something.	5	4	3	2	1
8. There is a narrow span of control.	5	4	3	2	1
9. For many tasks, there are no formal, written procedures.	1	2	3	4	5
10. One organizational goal is to be flexible and adaptable to change.	1	2	3	4	5
11. Managers move up on clear career ladders.	5	4	3	2	1
12. Promotion is based on technical competence.	5	4	3	2	1
13. Job designs facilitate opportunities to interact with workers from other departments.	1	2	3	4	5
14. For some situations, there are simply no rules or regulations.	5	4	3	2	1
15. There are few levels of authority.	1	2	3	4	5
16. Job duties and goals are not rigid and unchanging.	5	4	3	2	1
17. Temporary work teams are used to resolve problems or to accomplish goals.	1	2	3	4	5
18. Rules apply to everyone, no matter who you are.	5	4	3	2	1
19. Downward communication usually carries advice and information.	1	2	3	4	5
20. There is little upward communication.	5	4	3	2	1

Mechanistic/Organic Organization Survey Scoring Sheet

Transfer your numeric responses from the survey onto this scoring sheet. For example, your mechanistic score for Rules and Regulations is the sum of your responses to statements 5 and 18. Then, by addition, calculate the subtotals and the totals for both mechanistic and organic characteristics.

Category	Mechanistic		Organic	
Rules and Regulations	5	_____	2	_____
	18	_____	14	_____
Subtotals		_____		_____
Jobs and Roles	1	_____	9	_____
	16	_____	17	_____
Subtotals		_____		_____
Hierarchy	3	_____	6	_____
	8	_____	15	_____
Subtotals		_____		_____
Communication	7	_____	13	_____
	20	_____	19	_____
Subtotals		_____		_____
Culture	11	_____	4	_____
	12	_____	10	_____
Subtotals		_____		_____
TOTALS		_____		_____

On the Organization Continuum below, place an X for your mechanistic score and another X for your organic score.

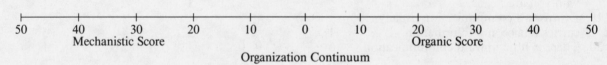

50	40	30	20	10	0	10	20	30	40	50

Mechanistic Score   Organic Score

Organization Continuum

130

Interpreting the Mechanistic/Organic Organization Survey Scores

Category	Interpretation	
	Mechanistic	*Organic*
Rules and Regulations	Many clear and precise rules and regulations that apply to everyone	A few flexible rules
Jobs and Roles	Specialized, rigid, and unchanging job duties and roles that are clearly defined for everyone	Few formal duties and procedures, while encouraging the use of temporary work teams
Hierarchy	Small spans of control and many levels of management arrayed in an orderly hierarchy; authority highly centralized	Large spans of control, few levels of management, and decentralized authority
Communication	Little upward communication, with downward communication primarily for the purpose of giving instructions on how to do things	Upward and horizontal communication or networking encouraged, with job design facilitating communication with workers from outside the group
Culture	A culture that maintains the status quo and breeds a company loyalty wherein managers move up a clearly defined career ladder based on demonstrated technical competence	A culture dedicated to flexibility and adaptability to change, with the philosophy that each worker should be encouraged to fully develop his/her talents and abilities

Exercise 11.2—Organizational Climate Questionnaire

PURPOSE

Help students gain an insight into the nature and elements of organizational climate

TIME REQUIRED

45 minutes

      Step 1: Individual activity (15 minutes)

      Step 2: Small-group activity (15 minutes)

      Step 3: Class discussion (15 minutes)

MATERIALS NEEDED

None

PROCEDURE

Step 1: Each student should complete and score the Organizational Climate Questionnaire on pp. 135–136. Students should think back to work or other organizational experiences and respond to each statement by circling the response that best fits their impression of the organization. If they have no such experience to draw on, they should respond to the statements by identifying those organizational characteristics they would prefer.

Step 2: The instructor will divide the class into small groups. Each group should compute its average scores for the subtotals and the total. Each person should give an example of a situation about which a strong feeling is held on one of the statements. The group should pick one of the examples to be shared with the whole class.

Step 3: A representative from each group will present the group-average scores and relate the example selected in Step 2.

Organizational Climate Questionnaire

Statement	Strongly Agree	Slightly Agree	Not Sure	Slightly Disagree	Strongly Disagree
1. Formal communication channels are not always used.	5	4	3	2	(1)
2. I am not always satisfied with my role in the organization.	1	2	3	4	(5)
3. It's not always clear as to who has the authority to make decisions.	5	4	3	2	(1)
4. Supervisors take the responsibility for seeing that the work is done properly.	1	2	3	4	(5)
5. Performance, not politics, is rewarded.	(5)	4	3	2	1
6. My role in the organization is pretty clear to me.	(5)	4	3	2	1
7. Most workers do not take responsibility for their work.	(1)	2	3	4	5
8. I wish I could get more feedback about how well I'm doing.	1	2	3	4	(5)
9. Everyone has a chance to express opinions on how to do things.	(5)	4	3	2	1
10. My rewards usually equal my contributions.	(5)	4	3	2	1
11. There are rules and regulations to cover every situation.	1	(2)	3	4	5
12. Supervisors seldom use positive encouragement to improve performance.	1	2	3	4	(5)
13. Most people understand my role in the organization.	(5)	4	3	2	1
14. Most people do what is asked of them and do it well.	(5)	4	3	2	1
15. Management respects the ideas and suggestions of the workers.	(5)	4	3	2	1
16. People believe that each worker should solve his/her own problems.	5	(4)	3	2	1
17. People are not allowed to communicate informally at all levels.	1	2	3	4	(5)
18. There is just too much red tape at work.	1	2	3	4	(5)
19. Most people don't understand my role on the job.	1	2	3	4	(5)
20. If you perform well, you will not necessarily receive appropriate rewards.	1	2	3	4	(5)

Organizational Climate Questionnaire Scoring Sheet

Transfer your numeric responses from the questionnaire onto this scoring sheet and sum the categories to find your subscores. For example, your Communication score is the sum of your responses to statements 1, 8, 15, and 17.

Communication	Role	Structure	Responsibility	Rewards
1 __1__	2 __5__	3 __1__	4 __5__	5 __5__
8 __5__	6 __5__	9 __5__	7 __1__	10 __5__
15 __5__	13 __5__	11 __2__	14 __5__	12 __5__
17 __5__	19 __5__	18 __5__	16 __4__	20 __5__
Totals __16__	__20__	__13__	__15__	__20__

Place an X on each of the five scales to mark your score.

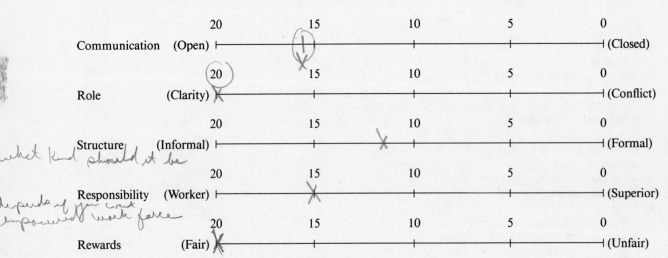

what kind should it be

depends if you went empowered work force

Place an X on the Organizational Climate Continuum below, to mark your total score of

_____ __84__ _____ .

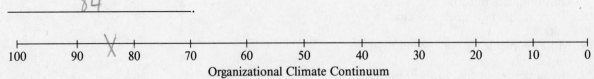

Organizational Climate Continuum

CHAPTER 12   MANAGING ORGANIZATION CHANGE

Exercise 12.1—Predicting Industry Change

PURPOSE

Help students gain a better insight into the forces for change that are reshaping the business world

TIME REQUIRED

45 minutes

> Step 1: Small-group research activity (completed before class)
> Step 2: Class discussion (45 minutes)

MATERIALS NEEDED

None

PROCEDURE

Step 1:   The instructor will divide the class into small groups and assign each group one of the following industries:

1. Airline
2. Automobile
3. Communications
4. Energy

5. Financial Services
6. Health and Personal Care
7. Housing
8. Leisure and Recreation

Using The Industry Change Identification Sheet on pp. 139–140, students are to identify changes and potential changes in the assigned industry.

Students may obtain the needed information from library business reference books, corporate annual reports, and key business periodicals. Information may also be obtained by interviews of people involved in the assigned industry.

Step 2:   A representative from each group will present the group's findings for discussion in class.

The Industry Change Identification Sheet

Industry Assigned: _____

	Current Changes	Predicted Changes

Input
Human Resources

Natural Resources

Technology

Environment
Competition

Suppliers

Government

139

	Current Changes	**Predicted Changes**
Customers	_____	_____
	_____	_____
	_____	_____
	_____	_____
	_____	_____

Exercise 12.2—Forces for Change

PURPOSE

Help students understand a framework for dealing with the forces of change

TIME REQUIRED

45 minutes

    Step 1: Individual activity (completed before class)
    Step 2: Small-group research activity (completed before class)
    Step 3: Class discussion (45 minutes)

MATERIALS NEEDED

None

PROCEDURE

Step 1:   Each student should study The Forces for Change Outline below.

THE FORCES FOR CHANGE OUTLINE

One of the frameworks for analyzing change requires identifying two different kinds of forces. First are the Driving Forces, or those forces that are instrumental in causing the change. Second are the Restraining Forces, or those forces that tend to maintain the status quo. Thus, change is generally seen as a slow process in which the Driving Forces overcome the Restraining Forces. At any point in time, the situation may seem to be somewhat stable with the two types of forces opposing each other in an unsteady balance, as follows:

Present Situation

Driving Forces | **Restraining Forces**

Efforts to manage the change process come down to the following actions:

1. promoting the change by facilitating the Driving Forces,
2. promoting the change by weakening or eliminating the Restraining Forces,

3. resisting the change by weakening or eliminating the Driving Forces,
4. resisting the change by facilitating the Restraining Forces, or
5. redirecting the change by manipulating the forces.

Step 2:   The instructor will divide the class into small groups and assign each group one of the following business changes:

1. Increased use of robotics
2. Concern for the quality of work
3. Early retirement
4. More women in the workplace
5. Shortage of skilled labor
6. Loss of the work ethic
7. Poor quality/workmanship in the workplace
8. Loss of American jobs to Japan and West Germany
9. Loss of American jobs to developing nations

For its assigned area of change, each group will conduct the library research necessary to complete The Change Analysis Sheet on pp. 143–144.

Step 3:   A representative from each group will present the group's findings for class discussion.

The Change Analysis Sheet

Assigned Change for Analysis: _____

Driving Forces: _____

_____

_____

_____

_____

_____

_____

_____

_____

_____

_____

_____

_____

_____

_____

_____

_____

Restraining Forces: _____

_____

_____

_____

_____

_____

_____

_____

_____

_____

_____

_____

_____

_____

_____

_____

_____

_____

Below, identify management efforts that might be used to manage the change.

1. Promote change by facilitating the Driving Forces: _____

_____

_____

_____

_____

_____

_____

2. Promote change by weakening or eliminating Restraining Forces: _____

_____

_____

_____

_____

_____

_____

3. Resist the change by weakening or eliminating the Driving Forces: _____

_____

_____

_____

_____

_____

_____

4. Resist the change by facilitating the Restraining Forces: _____

_____

_____

_____

_____

_____

_____

5. Redirect the change by manipulating the forces: _____

_____

_____

_____

_____

_____

_____

144

Exercise 12.3—Change at the State University

PURPOSE

Help students apply the concepts of change to a real-world institution

TIME REQUIRED

45 minutes

   Step 1: Individual activity (completed before class)
   Step 2: Small-group activity (30 minutes)
   Step 3: Class discussion (15 minutes)

MATERIALS NEEDED

None

PROCEDURE

Step 1:   Before class, each student should complete The University Change Identification Sheet on pp. 147–148 and study The Forces for Change Outline found in Exercise 12.2.

Step 2:   The instructor will divide the class into small groups. In each group, members will share their University Change Identification Sheets and select one major change for further analysis. That analysis will follow the process outlined on The University Change Analysis Sheet on pp. 149–150.

Step 3:   A representative from each group will present the group's findings for class discussion.

University Change Identification Sheet

In the spaces provided below, indicate the changes that are taking place at your university.

Current Changes

Input
Human Resources _____
_____
_____
_____
_____

Natural Resources _____
_____
_____
_____
_____

Technology _____
_____
_____
_____
_____

Environment
Competition _____
_____
_____
_____
_____

Suppliers _____
_____
_____
_____
_____

Government _____
_____
_____
_____
_____

Current Changes

Customers

_____

_____

_____

_____

_____

The University Change Analysis Sheet

Assigned Change for Analysis: _____

Driving Forces: _____

_____

_____

_____

_____

_____

_____

_____

_____

_____

_____

_____

_____

_____

_____

_____

_____

Restraining Forces: _____

_____

_____

_____

_____

_____

_____

_____

_____

_____

_____

_____

_____

_____

_____

_____

Below, identify management efforts that might be used to manage the change.

1. Promote change by facilitating the Driving Forces: _____

    _____

    _____

    _____

    _____

    _____

    _____

2. Promote change by weakening or eliminating Restraining Forces: _____

    _____

    _____

    _____

    _____

    _____

3. Resist the change by weakening or eliminating the Driving Forces: _____

    _____

    _____

    _____

    _____

    _____

    _____

4. Resist the change by facilitating the Restraining Forces: _____

    _____

    _____

    _____

    _____

    _____

5. Redirect the change by manipulating the forces: _____

    _____

    _____

    _____

    _____

    _____

CHAPTER 13   MANAGING HUMAN RESOURCES

Exercise 13.1—The Application Blank Exercise

PURPOSE

Help students develop a better understanding of equal opportunity and discriminatory practices in employment

TIME REQUIRED

45 minutes

> Step 1: Individual activity (completed before class)
> Step 2: Small-group activity (20 minutes)
> Step 3: Class discussion (25 minutes)

MATERIALS NEEDED

None

PROCEDURE

Step 1:   Before class, each student should complete The Slipshod Company Employment Application Blank Survey on pp. 153–154.

Step 2:   The instructor will divide the class into small groups. Each group will develop group responses to The Slipshod Company Employment Application Blank Survey.

Step 3:   A representative from each group will present the group's findings.

The Slipshod Company Employment Application Blank Survey

The following questions/statements were found on The Slipshod Company Employment Application Blank. For each item, indicate a numeric response, as follows:

1. If the item is legal, write a 1.
2. If the item's legality is marginal, write a 2.
3. If the item is definitely illegal, write a 3.

Provide a brief explanation for each response.

Item	Response	Explain
1. Include a photo	_____	
2. Name	_____	
3. Indicate Miss, Mrs., or Mr.	_____	
4. Alias	_____	
5. Address	_____	
6. Prior Addresses	_____	
7. Birthplace	_____	
8. Parents' Birthplace	_____	
9. Race	_____	
10. Color	_____	
11. Religion	_____	
12. National Origin	_____	
13. Marital Status	_____	

Item	Response	Explain
14. Family Status (Separated, Pregnant, etc.)	_____	_____ _____
15. Number and Ages of Dependents	_____	_____ _____
16. Height/Weight	_____	_____ _____
17. What Languages Spoken Fluently?	_____	_____ _____
18. Citizen of U.S.?	_____	_____ _____
19. Arrests/Convictions	_____	_____ _____
20. Own Your Car?	_____	_____ _____
21. Own Your Home?	_____	_____ _____
22. Handicaps?	_____	_____ _____
23. Organization Memberships	_____	_____ _____

154

Exercise 13.2—Using Graphic Rating Scales

PURPOSE

Help students understand the uses, advantages, and disadvantages of Graphic Rating Scales

TIME REQUIRED

45 minutes

     Step 1: Individual activity (completed before class)

     Step 2: Small-group activity (30 minutes)

     Step 3: Class discussion (15 minutes)

MATERIALS NEEDED

None

PROCEDURE

Step 1:   Before class, each student should review Figure 13.3, Graphic Rating Scales for a Bank Teller, and related text materials. Then each student should complete the Graphic Rating Scales for the Professor of This Class on p. 157.

Step 2:   The instructor will divide the class into small groups. Each group should share ideas on the Graphic Rating Scales for the Professor of This Class and then develop a group response to the Graphic Rating Scales for a Student in This Class on p. 159 that could be used by the instructor to evaluate the students. The group should also develop group responses to the discussion questions.

Step 3:   One representative from each group will present the group's findings and responses to the discussion questions.

QUESTIONS FOR DISCUSSION

1. Develop a system so that the Graphic Rating Scales for a Student in This Class could be used to assign course grades.
2. What are some advantages of Graphic Rating Scales?
3. What are some disadvantages of Graphic Rating Scales?

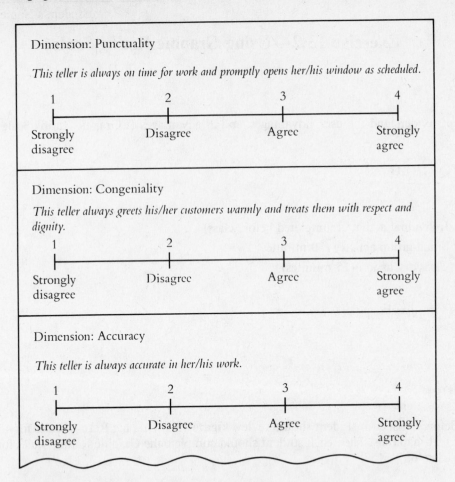

Dimension: Punctuality

This teller is always on time for work and promptly opens her/his window as scheduled.

1	2	3	4
Strongly disagree	Disagree	Agree	Strongly agree

Dimension: Congeniality

This teller always greets his/her customers warmly and treats them with respect and dignity.

1	2	3	4
Strongly disagree	Disagree	Agree	Strongly agree

Dimension: Accuracy

This teller is always accurate in her/his work.

1	2	3	4
Strongly disagree	Disagree	Agree	Strongly agree

FIGURE 13.3
Graphic Rating Scales for a Bank Teller (Reprinted from Ricky Griffin, *Management*, 3rd ed., p. 366. Copyright © Houghton Mifflin Company 1990. Used by permission.)

Graphic Rating Scales for the Professor of This Class

Dimension: _____

This Professor _____

	Strongly Agree 5	Agree 4	Not Sure 3	Disagree 2	Strongly Disagree 1

Dimension: _____

This Professor _____

	Strongly Agree 5	Agree 4	Not Sure 3	Disagree 2	Strongly Disagree 1

Dimension: _____

This Professor _____

	Strongly Agree 5	Agree 4	Not Sure 3	Disagree 2	Strongly Disagree 1

Dimension: _____

This Professor _____

	Strongly Agree 5	Agree 4	Not Sure 3	Disagree 2	Strongly Disagree 1

Dimension: _____

This Professor _____

	Strongly Agree 5	Agree 4	Not Sure 3	Disagree 2	Strongly Disagree 1

Dimension: _____

This Professor _____

	Strongly Agree 5	Agree 4	Not Sure 3	Disagree 2	Strongly Disagree 1

Divide the sum of the responses by the number of responses to calculate an average rating.

Sum of Responses _____ / Number of Responses _____ = _____ Average Rating

Graphic Rating Scales for a Student in This Class

Dimension: _____

This Student _____

	Strongly Agree 5	Agree 4	Not Sure 3	Disagree 2	Strongly Disagree 1

Dimension: _____

This Student _____

	Strongly Agree 5	Agree 4	Not Sure 3	Disagree 2	Strongly Disagree 1

Dimension: _____

This Student _____

	Strongly Agree 5	Agree 4	Not Sure 3	Disagree 2	Strongly Disagree 1

Dimension: _____

This Student _____

	Strongly Agree 5	Agree 4	Not Sure 3	Disagree 2	Strongly Disagree 1

Dimension: _____

This Student _____

	Strongly Agree 5	Agree 4	Not Sure 3	Disagree 2	Strongly Disagree 1

Dimension: _____

This Student _____

	Strongly Agree 5	Agree 4	Not Sure 3	Disagree 2	Strongly Disagree 1

Dimension: _____

This Student _____

	Strongly Agree 5	Agree 4	Not Sure 3	Disagree 2	Strongly Disagree 1

Exercise 13.3—Performance Appraisal

PURPOSE

Help students gain a better understanding of the complex problems involved in performance appraisal

TIME REQUIRED

45 minutes

Step 1: Individual activity (completed before class)

Step 2: Small-group activity (20 minutes)

Step 3: Class discussion (25 minutes)

MATERIALS NEEDED

None

PROCEDURE

Step 1: Each student should review the text materials on performance appraisal. Then each student should read The Problem at Bluefield and complete The Bluefield Performance Appraisal Worksheet on p. 163.

THE PROBLEM AT BLUEFIELD

Bob works for a fast-growing manufacturer of sporting goods at their oldest plant in Bluefield, West Virginia. Bob has an M.B.A. from State University and began his career at Bluefield in the Personnel Department. He got his first big chance when the company, facing increased problems with the local minority community, put Bob in charge of a new Affirmative Action Program. Bob is proud of his success in that position. His superiors were also impressed and promoted him to the position of Manager of Machine Operations. He managed a workforce of 74 employees through seven supervisors. He's held this job for only a year.

The plant is almost obsolete, the area is quite depressed, and the labor force is not well skilled. Top management has developed contingency plans for reducing the workforce at the plant or even shutting it down completely. If those events occur, Bob and some of his better subordinate supervisors will have the option of being transferred with promotions to a proposed new plant site in Sacramento, California.

It is time for the annual employee appraisal process, and the results will be used to: (1) distribute annual wage increases, and (2) make the pending personnel decisions on demotion, layoff, or promotion/transfer to the new plant. Bob has been allocated only $20,700 for pay increases for his seven supervisors, and he is told to allocate it all. Each supervisor in the plant is evaluated by a computer-based productivity program developed by Industrial Engineering. The program uses a wide variety of cost and output figures and calculates a Performance Measure (PM) for each supervisor on a scale ranging from 0 to 100.

Since Bob has never conducted a performance appraisal before, and because the outcome of this appraisal has such important implications, he is determined to do a good and fair job. Bob knows the following about the seven supervisors:

JOHN MILLER is the senior supervisor with 21 years of seniority. He is 60 years old and has only a sixth-grade education. His most recent PM score is 50, which is lower than it used to be. John's past appraisals suggest that he has done an average job in the past, and Bob thinks his performance is still average and is sorry to see John's performance declining. His peers are convinced that John is too old to cut the mustard. Bob thinks that John has the easiest job in the group. John is a widower who spends a lot of time at his cabin by the lake. His current salary is $45,000.

CHARLES GANTT is 52 with 16 years with the firm. His PM is 70 and his salary is $38,000. Charles is a high-school graduate, and his wife is quite wealthy. Bob believes that Charles has the best overall experience in the group and is a very capable supervisor, although his peers rank him average, the same as his past evaluations. Charles supervises a group that has about average responsibilities.

WILMA FORESTER is 36 with 10 years seniority. She has a B.S. in Management, a PM of 80, and a salary of $31,000. Bob feels she has one of the easier jobs and is doing only a so-so job. He is surprised to find that her earlier appraisals have been very good, an evaluation shared by her peers. Wilma's husband was killed in a car accident, and she has three dependent children.

TOM WILSON is 44 with 14 years with the company. Tom has a high-school diploma, a PM of 50, and a salary of $28,000. Tom has the hardest group to supervise, but his earlier appraisals have only been average, an opinion shared by Tom's peers. Bob agrees that Tom's performance is average and is concerned that it might get worse as Tom seems to be having too many personal problems lately.

SIDNEY BENTON is 35 and has 8 years of seniority, a PM of 80, and a salary of $26,000. Sidney has a B.S. in Industrial Technology and is enrolled in State's night MBA program. Sidney has a difficult job, requiring specialized skills, and he would be very hard to replace. Bob believes Sidney to be a top supervisor, an opinion shared by his peers. But Bob is troubled by past appraisals that vary from outstanding to poor.

ELMA THOMPSON is 32 with 5 years at the plant, a PM of only 30, and a salary of $22,000. She is a high-school drop-out, who quit school to have her first child. She is a single parent with four children and works very hard to support them. Elma represents one of the affirmative action promotions that Bob arranged when he was the Affirmative Action Officer, and he is disappointed to find that her past and present appraisals are quite poor. Although her present job is perceived to require average skill, her peers consider her to be an incompetent troublemaker who constantly complains about the need for more affirmative action efforts at the plant.

LUIS FUENTES is 26, has only 2 years with the company, a PM of only 20, and a salary of $19,000. He dropped out of school to take care of his sick mother and two younger sisters. Bob hired Luis as part of the Affirmative Action Program. Luis's first appraisal was low, but Bob believes that was because he was in a job requiring too much experience. So Bob moved him to a job with more average demands. Bob thinks that Luis is doing a bit better in the new job and, in time, will be a good supervisor. Peer evaluations are somewhat mixed but about average.

Step 2:   The instructor will divide the class into small groups. Each group is to develop an objective process for the performance evaluation and allocate the $20,700 accordingly. For each criterion used in the appraisal, each group should develop a written statement of justification.

Step 3:   A representative of each group will present the group's decisions to the class.

The Bluefield Performance Appraisal Worksheet

Your assignment is to identify and prioritize the appropriate performance appraisal criteria and develop an objective process for allocating the $20,700 and preparing for other potential personnel decisions.

Supervisor	Performance Appraisal Criteria	Raise
John Miller		
Charles Gantt		
Wilma Forester		
Tom Wilson		
Sidney Benton		
Elma Thompson		
Luis Fuentes		

CHAPTER 14   MOTIVATING EMPLOYEE PERFORMANCE

Exercise 14.1—Designing a Motivation Program

PURPOSE

Help students conceptualize the application of motivation theories to the motivation of employees

TIME REQUIRED

45 minutes

    Step 1: Individual activity (completed before class)

    Step 2: Small-group activity (25 minutes)

    Step 3: Class discussion (20 minutes)

MATERIALS NEEDED

None

PROCEDURE

Step 1:   Before class, each student should review The Problem at Bluefield (Exercise 13.3 on pp. 161–162), read The New Problem at Bluefield below, and complete the Need/Motivation Worksheet on p. 167.

THE NEW PROBLEM AT BLUEFIELD

Bob has just received some good news and some bad news. The good news is that top management has decided not to curtail operations at the Bluefield plant. The proposed relocation to the Sacramento site has been voted down by the Board of Directors. Thus, there is a new program to revitalize operations at Bluefield.

    The bad news is that Bob, because of his earlier success in the Personnel Department, has been assigned the task of developing a motivation plan for his seven subordinate supervisors. Bob decides to review the personnel files (see Exercise 13.3) and try to identify the needs or motivators for each supervisor. To provide a working framework for the study, Bob decides to use both Maslow's Need Hierarchy and Herzberg's Two-Factor Theory, as shown on the Need/Motivation Worksheet.

    Bob divides the worksheet into three sections: (1) Maslow's Needs; (2) Motivation Factors; and (3) Hygiene Factors. In each category, he plans to rank order the appropriate items for each supervisor, using a 1 for the top ranking, a 2 for the second ranking, etc..

Step 2:   The instructor will divide the class into small groups. Each group should arrive at a consensus on the Need/Motivation Worksheet and complete the Preliminary Motivation Plan Worksheet on p. 169.

Step 3:   Group representatives will present group findings for class discussion.

Need/Motivation Worksheet

(In each category, rank-order the appropriate items for each supervisor. Top rank = 1, Second rank = 2, etc.)

Need/Factor	John Miller	Charles Gantt	Wilma Forester	Tom Wilson	Sidney Benton	Elma Thompson	Luis Fuentes
Maslow's Needs Physiological							
Safety							
Belongingness							
Esteem							
Self-Actualization							
Motivation Factors Achievement							
Recognition							
Work Itself							
Responsibility							
Advancement/Growth							
Hygiene Factors Supervision							
Working Conditions							
Interpersonal							
Pay							
Security							
Policy & Administration							

The Preliminary Motivation Plan Worksheet

For each supervisor, select the most important item from the three categories (needs, motivation factors, hygiene factors) and recommend two things that Bob can do to effectively deal with that need or factor.

Supervisor	Top Need/Factor	Recommended Actions
John Miller	_____	1. _____
		2. _____
Charles Gantt	_____	1. _____
		2. _____
Wilma Forester	_____	1. _____
		2. _____
Tom Wilson	_____	1. _____
		2. _____
Sidney Benton	_____	1. _____
		2. _____
Elma Thompson	_____	1. _____
		2. _____
Luis Fuentes	_____	1. _____
		2. _____

Exercise 14.2—What Do Students Want from Their Jobs?

PURPOSE

Help students deal with the problem of job values and what they seek in a career job

TIME REQUIRED

45 minutes

Step 1: Individual activity (completed before class)

Step 2: Small-group activity (30 minutes)

Step 3: Class discussion (15 minutes)

MATERIALS NEEDED

None

PROCEDURE

Step 1: Before class, each student should complete the Job Values Survey on p. 173.

JOB VALUES SURVEY INSTRUCTIONS

1. What do you want from your career job? Respond in Column 1 by ranking the following 14 job values (1 is tops, 14 is last).

2. Would men or women rank this job value higher? Respond in Column 2 by placing an M if you think men rank it higher or a W if you think women rank it higher.

3. Would recruiters from employing institutions, when asked how students rank this value, rank it higher or lower than students? Respond in Column 3 with a + (plus) if you think recruiters rank it higher than students or with a − (minus) if you think recruiters rank it lower.

4. Would your business professors, when asked how students rank this value, rank it higher or lower than students? Respond in Column 4 with a + if you think professors rank it higher than students or with a − if you think professors rank it lower.

Step 2: The instructor will divide the class into small groups. Each group will compute a group-average ranking for each value and complete the rest of the Job Values Survey.

Step 3: Group representatives will make group reports to the class for discussion.

Job Values Survey

Job Value	Column 1 Your Ranking	Column 2 Sex M or W	Column 3 Recruiter + or −	Column 4 Professor + or −
Working Conditions	_____	_____	_____	_____
Work with People	_____	_____	_____	_____
Fringe Benefits	_____	_____	_____	_____
Challenge	_____	_____	_____	_____
Location of Job	_____	_____	_____	_____
Self-Development	_____	_____	_____	_____
Type of Work	_____	_____	_____	_____
Job Title	_____	_____	_____	_____
Training Programs	_____	_____	_____	_____
Advancement	_____	_____	_____	_____
Salary	_____	_____	_____	_____
Company Reputation	_____	_____	_____	_____
Job Security	_____	_____	_____	_____
Freedom on the Job	_____	_____	_____	_____

CHAPTER 15 LEADERSHIP AND INFLUENCE PROCESSES

Exercise 15.1—Occupational Power Bases

PURPOSE

Help students learn to identify the power bases that typify certain occupations

TIME REQUIRED

45 minutes

Step 1: Individual activity (10 minutes)
Step 2: Small-group activity (20 minutes)
Step 3: Class discussion (15 minutes)

MATERIALS NEEDED

None

PROCEDURE

Step 1: Each student should complete the Power Base Worksheet on p. 177 and the Power Base Analysis Worksheet on pp. 179–181.

Step 2: The instructor will divide the class into small groups. Each group will achieve consensus in their responses to the Power Base Worksheet and the Power Base Analysis Worksheet.

Step 3: A representative from each group will present the group's responses for class discussion.

Power Base Worksheet

For each occupation, place an "X" for each power base that the person probably possesses in that job.

Occupation	Legitimate Power	Reward Power	Coercive Power	Referent Power	Expert Power
University Professor	_____	_____	_____	_____	_____
Homemaker	_____	_____	_____	_____	_____
CEO of a Bank	_____	_____	_____	_____	_____
City Mayor	_____	_____	_____	_____	_____
Secretary	_____	_____	_____	_____	_____
Barber	_____	_____	_____	_____	_____
U.S. Marines Drill Instructor	_____	_____	_____	_____	_____

Power Base Analysis Worksheet

For each occupation, provide an explanation or example of each power base associated with that job.

University Professor

Legitimate Power: _____

_____

Reward Power: _____

_____

Coercive Power: _____

_____

Referent Power: _____

_____

Expert Power: _____

_____

Homemaker

Legitimate Power: _____

_____

Reward Power: _____

_____

Coercive Power: _____

_____

Referent Power: _____

_____

Expert Power: _____

_____

CEO of a Bank

Legitimate Power: _____

_____

Reward Power: _____

_____

Coercive Power: _____

_____

Referent Power: _____

_____

Expert Power: _____

_____

City Mayor

Legitimate Power: _____
_____

Reward Power: _____
_____

Coercive Power: _____
_____

Referent Power: _____
_____

Expert Power: _____
_____

Secretary

Legitimate Power: _____
_____

Reward Power: _____
_____

Coercive Power: _____
_____

Referent Power: _____
_____

Expert Power: _____
_____

Barber

Legitimate Power: _____
_____

Reward Power: _____
_____

Coercive Power: _____
_____

Referent Power: _____
_____

Expert Power: _____
_____

U.S. Marines Drill Instructor

Legitimate Power: _____

_____

Reward Power: _____

_____

Coercive Power: _____

_____

Referent Power: _____

_____

Expert Power: _____

_____

Exercise 15.2—Identifying Leadership Traits

PURPOSE

Help students gain insights into the difficulty of verifying leadership trait theories

TIME REQUIRED

45 minutes

      Step 1: Individual activity (10 minutes)

      Step 2: Small-group activity (20 minutes)

      Step 3: Class discussion (15 minutes)

MATERIALS NEEDED

None

PROCEDURE

Step 1: Each student should read the Trait Theory Problem Introduction below and complete the Leadership Traits Worksheet on p. 185.

TRAIT THEORY PROBLEM INTRODUCTION

For years, theorists have proposed that there are certain personal traits that all or most leaders share in common. Some experts have advanced the great man theory that stipulates that all great people possessed some fundamental trait or set of traits that differentiated them from other people. The Leadership Traits Worksheet on page 185 lists some of those traits. The worksheet also lists eight great leaders. For each of these leaders, you are to rank-order the top five leadership traits for which that particular leader is remembered.

Step 2: The instructor will divide the class into small groups. Each group will achieve consensus on group responses to the Leadership Traits Worksheet and the discussion questions.

Step 3: A representative of each group will present the group's responses for class discussion.

QUESTIONS FOR DISCUSSION

1. Were all of these people really leaders? If not, who was not?
2. Were some of the leadership traits common to all or most of the leaders?
3. Did the group have difficulty agreeing on some traits? Which ones? For which leaders?
4. What would account for the differences in individual group-member perceptions of leaders and their traits?

Leadership Traits Worksheet

For each leader, rank-order the top five (1, 2, 3, 4, 5) leadership traits for which he/she will be remembered.

Trait	Jesus Christ	Mohandas Ghandi	Mikhail Gorbachev	Adolf Hitler	Ayatollah Khomeini	Martin Luther King, Jr.	Richard Nixon	Corazon Aquino
Above-Average Height	___	___	___	___	___	___	___	___
Assertiveness	___	___	___	___	___	___	___	___
Attractiveness	___	___	___	___	___	___	___	___
Charisma	___	___	___	___	___	___	___	___
Communication Skills	___	___	___	___	___	___	___	___
Courage	___	___	___	___	___	___	___	___
Intelligence	___	___	___	___	___	___	___	___
Open-Mindedness	___	___	___	___	___	___	___	___
People-Orientation	___	___	___	___	___	___	___	___
Perseverance	___	___	___	___	___	___	___	___
Self-Confidence	___	___	___	___	___	___	___	___
Task-Orientation	___	___	___	___	___	___	___	___
Truthfulness	___	___	___	___	___	___	___	___

CHAPTER 16 MANAGING INTERPERSONAL AND GROUP PROCESSES

Exercise 16.1—Nominations: Personal Instrumented Feedback

PURPOSE

Provide feedback to group members on how they are perceived by each other

Analyze the climate and the norms of the group by studying members' behavior, composition of the group, and members' expectations of each other

TIME REQUIRED

60 minutes

MATERIALS NEEDED

None

PROCEDURE

Select one of the following instruments:

   Learning-Climate Analysis Form
   Group-Behavior Questionnaire
   Intentions and Choices Inventory

Each of the forms focuses on some aspect of group-member behavior which the facilitator may wish to discuss. This general process is suggested for each inventory.

Step 1: The facilitator discusses goals and distributes copies of the form selected. Participants fill out the form individually.

Step 2: As soon as members finish, they share their nominations of each other. (When the Learning-Climate Analysis Form is used, members also try to reach a consensus on each nomination.) Whenever possible, the person nominating specifies the incidents that led him/her to make that nomination.

Step 3: The group members discuss the impact of the feedback on themselves.

Step 4: The group analyzes the effects of its members' behavior on the group. During this phase, the facilitator may wish to offer theories relating to climate, norms, and group composition.

Step 5: Group members are urged to try, in later meetings, new behavior which reflects the results of this exercise.

Reprinted from: *A Handbook of Structured Experiences for Human Relations Training* [Vol. III], San Diego, CA: Pfeiffer & Company, 1974. Used with permission.

Learning-Climate Analysis Form

Introduction: Learning about one's self, others, and groups is easier when group members feel free to be themselves; they contribute most to the group when they are most themselves, and they offer least when they are confined to one role.

People seem most free to be themselves when the level of trust in a group is high: Defensiveness is reduced, manipulative strategies tend to disappear, and the flow of information is increased. Instead, when the level of trust is low, people tend to be defensive, to adopt manipulative strategies, and to withhold information about themselves.

A high trust level seems to be encouraged when there is an increase in awareness, self-acceptance, acceptance of others, and problem-centering.

The purpose of this experience is to examine some of the dimensions of trust levels and to determine their effect on your group.

Instructions:

1. Read each definition.
2. Indicate which member you believe most closely resembles the description.
3. When everyone has finished, compare nominations for each of the dimensions.
4. Using the method of group consensus, select the one person who is most representative of each dimension.
5. Discuss what might be done to increase the trust level.

Definitions: A person may be said to be . . .

1. *Aware* when his outward behavior reflects his inner feelings and thoughts; when he explicitly recognizes how his feelings are influencing his behavior; when he recognizes and responds to feelings he experiences. Awareness may be indicated by a statement such as "I feel somewhat at a loss; we don't have a topic" (instead of "We're just floundering without something we can get our teeth into"). Or by "I'm not sure I want to say how I feel about you" (instead of "I don't think we ought to get personal").

   Your nomination _____ Consensus _____

2. *Self-accepting* when he is able to accept his own feelings without denying them, giving rationalizations for them, or apologizing for them. Self-acceptance may be evidenced by a statement such as "I'm bored with what you are saying" (instead of "This is a boring topic"). Or by "I'm angry at myself for being ineffective" (instead of "This group is not getting anywhere").

   Your nomination _____ Consensus _____

3. *Accepting of others* when he is able to accept the feelings and thoughts of others without trying to change them; when he is able to let others be themselves even though they are different from him. Acceptance of others may be shown by listening in order to understand; by listening without trying to refute; by trying not to argue; by asking questions in order to understand; or by not judging another.

   Your nomination _____ Consensus _____

4. *Supportive* when he seeks ways to help others reach goals that are important to them; when he tries to understand what others want to do, although he may not agree with their conclusions; or when he encourages others to try behavior new to them. Supportiveness may be seen in comments such as "Could you tell me how I might help you reach your objective" or "I am not sure I agree with what you are proposing, but I support your effort to get something going" or "Let me see if I understand what you want us to do."

Your nomination _____ Consensus _____

5. *Risk-taking* when he goes "beyond the known" by experimenting with new behavior; when he wants to accomplish something or to support someone else more than he wants to play it safe or to keep his cool; when he is willing to risk being angry, anxious, caring, driving, or retreating, even though these behaviors may make him appear foolish or inept or unintelligent or may arouse his anxiety. Risk-taking may be shown by initiating feedback on one's behavior or by supporting someone when it is not clear what the consequences will be or by giving feedback to others on their behavior.

Your nomination _____ Consensus _____

6. *Problem-centered* when he focuses on problems facing a group rather than on control or method; when he tries to learn by solving problems himself rather than by using someone else's solutions. Problem-centering may be seen in one's efforts to find out what is blocking a group, to increase personal effectiveness, and to probe beyond the symptoms. Problem-centering assumes that more work gets done when individuals and groups learn how to solve problems than when they maintain the same pattern of method, control, leadership, or feedback.

Your nomination _____ Consensus _____

7. *Leveling* when he is able to be open about his feelings and thoughts; when his outward behavior reflects his inner experience.

Your nomination _____ Consensus _____

Group-Behavior Questionnaire

Instructions: Answer all questions with the *first names only* of two group members. Base your nominations on interactions in the group. Be sure to choose *two* people for each question. *Do not include yourself.*

1. Which members can most easily influence others to change their opinions? _____ _____

2. Which are least able to influence others to change their opinions? _____ _____

3. Which have clashed most sharply with others in the course of the meetings? _____ _____

4. Which are most highly accepted by the group? _____ _____

5. Which are most ready to support members? _____ _____

6. Which try to keep themselves in the limelight? _____ _____

7. Which are most likely to put personal goals above group goals? _____ _____

8. Which have most often introduced topics not directly related to the group task? _____ _____

9. Which have shown the greatest desire to accomplish something? _____ _____

10. Which have wanted to avoid conflict in group discussions? _____ _____

11. Which tend to withdraw from active discussion when strong differences begin to appear? _____ _____

12. Which have sought to help in the resolution of differences between others? _____ _____

13. Which have wanted the group to be warm, friendly, and comfortable? _____ _____

14. Which have competed most with others? _____ _____

15. Which have done most to keep the group lively? _____ _____

16. Which would you choose to work with? _____ _____

17. With which have you talked least? _____ _____

Intentions and Choices Inventory

Instructions: In the spaces below, put the names of the two individuals in your group who seem to fit best each of the descriptions. You may include yourself.

Intentions

1. He seems to be *aware* of his intentions and is able to communicate them without ambiguity; others are seldom in doubt about what his intentions are with respect to issues and group process.

   _____   _____

2. His intentions are *partially clear,* although there is some ambiguity; others are not always certain what this person intends with respect to issues and group process.

   _____   _____

3. His intentions are *derivable only by inference;* others can infer from his behavior what this person intends, but his intentions are not communicated.

   _____   _____

4. His intentions are *unclear;* others do not know where this person stands on issues or on group process.

   _____   _____

Choices

5. He seems to have a range of choices available in different situations; he does not simply react to outside signals but chooses his own path.

   _____   _____

6. He seems to want to make more choices but finds difficulty in doing much more than reacting.

   _____   _____

7. He seems to want others to make choices for him and for the group; he does not introduce his own preferences until he hears what a number of others say.

   _____   _____

8. He seems uncomfortable about making choices; he seems to prefer not to have to choose, and he is unhappy with situations in which he must do so.

   _____   _____

Exercise 16.2—The Fishbone

PURPOSE

Help students learn to use the fishbone technique, a popular tool of Japanese quality circles

TIME REQUIRED

45 minutes

Step 1: Individual activity (completed before class)

Step 2: Small-group activity (25 minutes)

Step 3: Class discussion (20 minutes)

MATERIALS NEEDED

None

PROCEDURE

Step 1: Before class, each student should study The Fishbone Instruction Sheet.

THE FISHBONE INSTRUCTION SHEET

Japanese quality circles often use the fishbone "cause and effect" graphic technique to initiate the resolution of a group work problem. The fishbone technique is usually accomplished in the following six steps:

1. Write the problem in the "head" of the fish (the large block).
2. Brainstorm the major causes of the problem and list them on the fish "bones."
3. Analyze each main cause, and write in minor subcauses on bone subbranches.
4. Reach consensus on one or two of the major causes of the problem.
5. Explore ways to correct or remove the major cause(s).
6. Prepare a report or presentation explaining the proposed change.

The completed fishbone will look something like this:

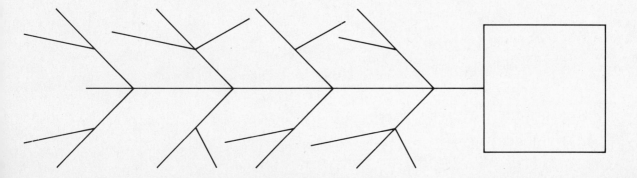

Step 2:   The instructor will divide the class into small groups. Each group will be given one of the following problems to analyze, using The Fishbone Worksheet on pp. 197–198.

1. Student parking on campus is inadequate.

2. Computer equipment available for student use is inadequate.

3. Required business courses are not offered at different, more flexible times.

4. There are too few upper-division business elective courses offered.

5. There are not enough sections of required business courses offered to meet student demand.

6. Some business courses have too many students in them to facilitate optimum learning.

7. Faculty are not available for student consultation/assistance.

8. There is inadequate opportunity for students to receive good course requirement/scheduling counseling.

9. Students have inadequate communication skills (both written and oral).

10. Some courses have too much theory without opportunity for real-world application.

Step 3:   A representative from each group will present the group's fishbone analysis.

The Fishbone Worksheet[1]

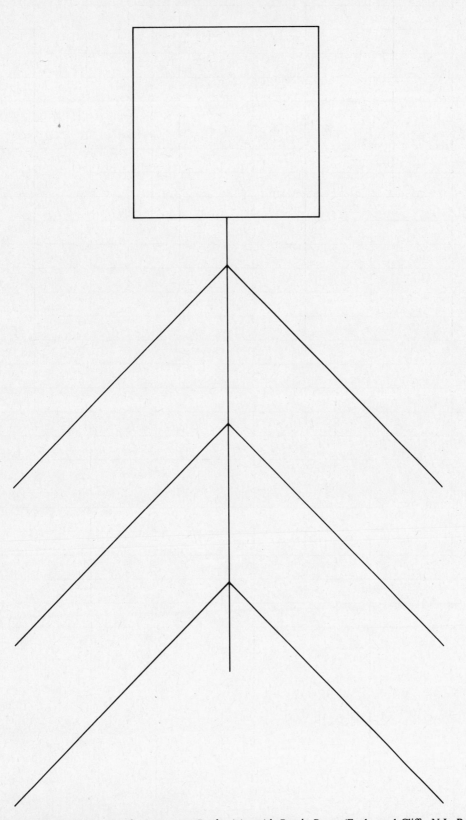

1. Sud Ingle, *Quality Circles Master Guide: Increasing Productivity with People Power* (Englewood Cliffs, N.J.: Prentice-Hall, 1982), pp. 110–112. Reprinted by permission of the author.

The *major* cause(s):_____

_____

_____

_____

_____

Possible corrective actions:_____

_____

_____

_____

_____

_____

_____

_____

_____

_____

_____

_____

The group's proposal:_____

_____

_____

_____

_____

CHAPTER 17 MANAGING COMMUNICATION IN ORGANIZATIONS

Exercise 17.1—A Communication Skills Survey

PURPOSE

Help students understand the characteristics of a good communicator while gaining insights into their own communication skills

TIME REQUIRED

45 minutes

    Step 1: Individual activity (15 minutes)

    Step 2: Small-group activity (15 minutes)

    Step 3: Class discussion (15 minutes)

MATERIALS NEEDED

None

PROCEDURE

Step 1: Each student should complete and score the Communication Skills Survey (pp. 201–202). Students should think back to work or other organizational experiences and respond to each statement by circling the response that best fits their attitudes and behaviors.

Step 2: The instructor will divide the class into small groups. Each group should compute its average scores for the subtotals and the total. For each communication skill subgroup, the group should develop a list of five things a person can do to improve his/her score in that subgroup.

Step 3: A representative from each group will present the group's findings for class discussion.

Communication Skills Survey

Statement	Strongly Agree	Slightly Agree	Not Sure	Slightly Disagree	Strongly Disagree
1. When responding, I try to use specific details or examples	5	4	3	2	1
2. I tend to talk more than others.	1	2	3	4	5
3. If the other person seems not to understand me, I try to speak more slowly and more distinctly.	5	4	3	2	1
4. I tend to forget that some words have many meanings.	1	2	3	4	5
5. When I give feedback, I respond to the facts and keep the feelings out of it.	1	2	3	4	5
6. I am not embarrassed by periods of silence when I'm talking to someone.	5	4	3	2	1
7. I concentrate hard to avoid distracting nonverbal cues.	5	4	3	2	1
8. Listening and hearing are the same things.	1	2	3	4	5
9. I make sure the person wants feedback before I give it.	5	4	3	2	1
10. I avoid saying "Good," "Go on," etc. while the other person is speaking.	5	4	3	2	1
11. I try to delay giving feedback so I can have more time to think it through.	1	2	3	4	5
12. I enjoy using slang and quaint local expressions.	1	2	3	4	5
13. My feedback focuses on how the other person can use my ideas.	5	4	3	2	1
14. Body language is important for speakers, not listeners.	1	2	3	4	5
15. I use technical jargon only when talking to experts.	5	4	3	2	1
16. When someone is wrong, I make sure he knows it.	1	2	3	4	5
17. I try to express my ideas in general, overall terms.	1	2	3	4	5
18. When I'm listening, I try not to be evaluative.	5	4	3	2	1

Communication Skills Survey Scoring Sheet

Transfer your numeric responses from the survey onto this scoring sheet and sum the categories and total. For instance, your Feedback Skill score is the sum of your responses to statements 1, 5, 9, 11, 13, and 16.

Feedback Skill	Listening Skill	Articulation Skill
1 _____	2 _____	3 _____
5 _____	6 _____	4 _____
9 _____	8 _____	7 _____
11 _____	10 _____	12 _____
13 _____	14 _____	15 _____
16 _____	18 _____	17 _____
Subtotals _____	_____	_____
Total _____		

Place an X on each of the three continuums to mark your subtotals.

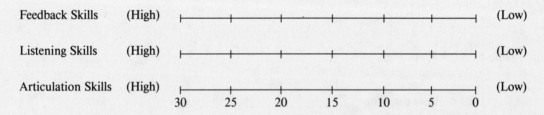

Feedback Skills   (High) ├───┼───┼───┼───┼───┤ (Low)

Listening Skills   (High) ├───┼───┼───┼───┼───┤ (Low)

Articulation Skills (High) ├───┼───┼───┼───┼───┤ (Low)
                            30   25   20   15   10   5   0

Place an X on the Communication Skills Continuum below to mark your total score.

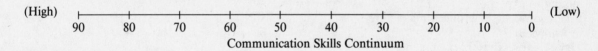

(High) ├───┼───┼───┼───┼───┼───┼───┼───┤ (Low)
       90   80   70   60   50   40   30   20   10   0
            Communication Skills Continuum

Exercise 17.2—The Letter of Justification

PURPOSE

Help students understand the temptation for some people to use technical jargon and help them appreciate how little such jargon may actually contribute to clear communications

TIME REQUIRED

45 minutes

Step 1: Individual activity (20 minutes)

Step 2: Small-group activity (15 minutes)

Step 3: Class discussion (10 minutes)

MATERIALS NEEDED

None

PROCEDURE

Step 1: Each student should read The Letter of Justification Problem Situation and write the required letter of justification.

THE LETTER OF JUSTIFICATION PROBLEM SITUATION

You are an office worker in a local bank branch office and you have a serious communication overload problem. A Japanese computer salesman has just shown you an innovative new lap-top personal computer that will solve your communication problems. Unfortunately, the computer is extremely expensive and you must justify such a high-dollar request to Randall Radcliff, the vice president of purchasing, who is officed in San Diego. Your earlier efforts to justify expenditures through him have failed.

You are in the process of writing a letter of justification to Mr. Radcliff when you realize that you don't have enough technical knowledge to explain why this particular piece of equipment can do things your present PC cannot do. Then a friend shows you the Gobbledygook Systematic Buzz Phrase Generator. For each justifying sentence in your letter, you can simply think of one or more three-digit numbers and insert the corresponding buzz words from the three columns on the phrase generator. For instance, the number 238 generates the phrase "systematized reciprocal hardware."

Each student should write a letter of justification using the Gobbledygook Systematic Buzz Phrase Generator on p. 204.

Step 2: The instructor will divide the class into small groups. Each group should share letters, pick one to share with the class, and develop group responses to the discussion questions.

Step 3: Each group representative will present the group's letter selection and responses to the discussion questions.

GOBBLEDYGOOK SYSTEMATIC BUZZ PHRASE GENERATOR[1]

Simply think of a three-digit number and select the corresponding buzz words from the three columns shown below.

Column 1	Column 2	Column 3
0. integrated	0. management	0. options
1. total	1. organizational	1. flexibility
2. systematized	2. monitored	2. capability
3. parallel	3. reciprocal	3. mobility
4. functional	4. digital	4. programming
5. responsive	5. logic	5. concept
6. optical	6. transitional	6. time-phase
7. synchronized	7. incremental	7. projection
8. compatible	8. third-generation	8. hardware
9. balanced	9. policy	9. contingency

QUESTIONS FOR DISCUSSION

1. What problems can technical jargon cause for the receiving individual? For the organization?
2. Is the use of technical jargon universally bad? If not, when is it an aid to the communication process?

---

1. Reprinted from William V. Haney, *Communication and Interpersonal Relations: Text and Cases,* 5th ed., 1986, p. 272. By permission of Richard D. Irwin, Inc.

Exercise 17.3—Comparing One-Way and Two-Way Communication

PURPOSE

Help students understand the relative advantages and disadvantages of one-way and two-way communication

TIME REQUIRED

45 minutes

    Step 1: Instructions (10 minutes)
    Step 2: Communication experiments (20 minutes)
    Step 3: Class discussion (15 minutes)

MATERIALS NEEDED

None

PROCEDURE

Step 1: Students will be required to draw a diagram in each of two experiments, using the Experiment 1 Worksheet (p. 207) and then the Experiment 2 Worksheet (p. 209). Both diagrams can be drawn using circles, semicircles, triangles, and squares.

Step 2: One student is selected to be the facilitator for both experiments. Another student will be asked to serve as timer.

EXPERIMENT 1

The instructor will give the facilitator the Instruction Sheet for Experiment 1. The facilitator will take the instructions into the hall for a few minutes to prepare for the experiment. When called in by the professor, the timer will note the starting time, and the facilitator will stand with his/her back to the class, holding the instructions so that students cannot see them. The facilitator will then give the students the instructions necessary to draw the diagram. Only verbal, one-way communication can be used. Students are to remain quiet and listen. When the last instruction has been given, the timer will record the time.

EXPERIMENT 2

The instructor will give the facilitator the Instruction Sheet for Experiment 2. The facilitator will take the instructions into the hall for a few minutes to prepare for the experiment. When called in by the professor, the timer will record the time and the facilitator will stand facing the group. Instructions will be communicated in a two-way process, using only verbal communication. That is, students are encouraged to allow the instructions to continue until each student is absolutely certain that instructions to that point are clear. When the task is completed, the timer should record the time.

SCORING

The facilitator will then draw both diagrams on the board. Each student will report the number of correct figures drawn in each experiment, and class averages will be computed. The timer will report the time required for each experiment.

	Experiment 1	Experiment 2
Correct Figures:		
On your sheet	_____	_____
Class average	_____	_____
Time Required	_____	_____

Step 3:   The class will discuss the results.

QUESTIONS FOR DISCUSSION

1. How did you feel during the one-way process? The two-way process?
2. Ask the facilitator how he/she felt during the one-way process? The two-way process?
3. Which method produced the most accurate results?
4. Which method required the most time?
5. When should a manager use one-way communication?
6. When should a manager use two-way communication?

Experiment 1 Worksheet

Using circles, semicircles, triangles, and squares, draw the six connecting figures below. You are not permitted to speak.

Experiment 2 Worksheet

Using circles, semicircles, triangles, and squares, draw the six connecting figures below. Do not let the facilitator go to the next figure until you are sure you understand the instructions to that point.

CHAPTER 18   THE NATURE OF CONTROL

Exercise 18.1—University Control Systems

PURPOSE

Help students understand the application of control systems

TIME REQUIRED

45 minutes

    Step 1: Small-group activity (25 minutes)
    Step 2: Class discussion (20 minutes)

MATERIALS NEEDED

None

PROCEDURE

Step 1:   The instructor will divide the class into small groups. Each group will study The University Control Problem that follows, complete The University Control Matrix (p. 213), and develop group responses to the discussion questions.

THE UNIVERSITY CONTROL PROBLEM

You are a committee appointed by the State University Student Council to help the new President deal with a number of problems that have plagued the campus for years. For example, the University regularly runs out of funds before the academic year ends, causing major disruptions of student services. In fact, some departments seem to have no knowledge of how much money they need or how much they have spent. Students are upset because tuition fees are constantly being changed in an effort to match the university's varying demands for money. Department chairs have no idea how many students are being admitted, so they never schedule the appropriate number of courses. Some buildings are in bad physical shape. Classrooms are assigned to departments, and some classrooms seem to sit empty while others are overcrowded. There seems to be an oversupply of research equipment but a shortage of computer equipment for students. Some schools, such as the business school, don't have enough faculty to teach their classes, while some departments in liberal arts have surplus faculty with no students to teach.

Your committee has decided to approach the problem by using The University Control Matrix, which facilitates the identification of controls needed for the University's four categories of resources—physical, financial, human, and information.

Controls are divided into three categories. First are the Preliminary Controls that control inputs into the University. Second are the Screening Controls that control the University's transformation processes. Third are the Postaction Controls that control the outputs of the University's systems.

The committee's job is to complete The University Control Matrix by identifying the different controls that might be established for each of the four resources at each of the three system stages.

Step 2:   A representative from each group will present the group's findings for class discussion.

QUESTIONS FOR DISCUSSION

1. Which of the recommended controls may be the hardest to implement? To manage?
2. Will the controls receive some forms of resistance? If so, explain.

The University Control Matrix

System Stages	Physical Resources	Financial Resources	Human Resources	Information Resources
Preliminary Controls				
Screening Controls				
Postaction Controls				

213

Exercise 18.2—Establishing Organizational Control Systems

PURPOSE

Help students understand how control systems are integrated into an organization's overall operating system

TIME REQUIRED

45 minutes

> Step 1: Small-group activity (25 minutes)
> Step 2: Class discussion (20 minutes)

MATERIALS NEEDED

None

PROCEDURE

Step 1: The instructor will divide the class into small groups. Each group will analyze The Control Problem Situation below, complete The Control System Matrix (p. 217), and develop group responses to the discussion questions.

THE CONTROL PROBLEM SITUATION

You work for a small but growing manufacturer of lawn and hedge trimmers. The organization has grown quickly, and management has not had time to study the problem of controls. Management has asked you to develop a plan for establishing organizational control systems.

You have decided to begin your task by completing The Control System Matrix, which requires the identification of controls needed for the organization's four categories of resources—physical, financial, human, and information.

The required controls are divided into three categories. First are the Preliminary Controls, which control inputs into the organizational systems. Second are the Screening Controls, which control the organizational transformation processes. Third are the Postaction Controls, which control the outputs of the organizational systems.

Your task is to complete The Control System Matrix by identifying the different controls that might be established for each of the four resources at each of the three system stages.

Step 2: A representative from each group will present the group's findings for class discussion.

QUESTIONS FOR DISCUSSION

1. Which of the four organizational resources (physical, financial, human, and information) is the most central for the organizational control system? Why?
2. Which of the four organizational resources has the least objective control methods? Why?

The Control System Matrix

System Stages	Physical Resources	Financial Resources	Human Resources	Information Resources
Preliminary Controls				
Screening Controls				
Postaction Controls				

217

CHAPTER 19 MANAGING QUALITY, PRODUCTIVITY, AND OPERATIONS

Exercise 19.1—Using the Gantt Chart

PURPOSE

Help students understand the use and application of Gantt charts in operations management

TIME REQUIRED

45 minutes

Step 1: Small-group activity (30 minutes)
Step 2: Class discussion (15 minutes)

MATERIALS NEEDED

None

PROCEDURE

Step 1: The instructor will divide the class into small groups. Each group will read The On-Time Producer's Problem Situation that follows, complete the Gantt Chart (p. 221), and develop responses to the discussion questions.

THE ON-TIME PRODUCER'S PROBLEM SITUATION

You are the members of the On-Time Producer's Scheduling Team. Your job is to manage work schedules and report to top management at the weekly staff meetings held every Monday morning. The company has two unwavering policies: (1) we always ship on schedule, and (2) we never work overtime. The factory works one 8-hour shift 5 days a week.

You came in early today, May 15, to prepare for the weekly staff meeting. Of concern is the important order from the Hot-Shot Corporation, on which you have collected the following information:

1. The order resulted in a schedule of eight sequential tasks (that is, a task cannot begin until the preceding task is complete), as shown at the top of the next page:

Sequence No.	Task Activity	Days Required to Complete
1	Design change	3
2	Prepare blueprints	2
3	Purchase materials	6
4	Manufacture parts	12
5	Assemble	3
6	Paint	1
7	Test	1
8	Package	1

2. The Manufacture parts activity includes the manufacturing of five detail parts, which can be made independently within the 12-day period:

Detail Parts	Days Required
Frames	12
Flanges	10
Handles	10
Gears	5
Guides	2

3. The design change task began on May 1, and the order is to be packaged for shipment on June 8.

4. Engineering finished its task in just two days.

5. Blueprinting began on May 3 and took three days because of an equipment breakdown.

6. Material purchases were initiated on May 8 and were finished one day ahead of schedule on May 12.

7. Parts manufacture is scheduled to start tomorrow, although you could begin today.

At last week's staff meeting, top management announced that Gantt charts would be used to schedule and monitor work in the shops. Furthermore, updated Gantt charts were to be used as part of the staff meeting reports. All you know about Gantt charts is that they are graphic techniques applied to operations scheduling.

Your task for today's staff meeting is to apply the above data to the construction of a Gantt Chart on page 221.

Step 2:   A representative from each group will present the group's findings for class discussion.

QUESTIONS FOR DISCUSSION

1. Just before you are to attend the Monday, May 15 staff meeting, you get a call from Jim Mueller, Maintenance Chief, who tells you that he would like to perform the company's annual equipment maintenance inspection on the following Monday. This means that most of the equipment will be taken out of use for a good part of that day. In fact, for last year's annual inspection, some of the equipment was down for almost two full days. What would your response be?

2. Is there a better way to do the annual equipment maintenance inspection?

Gantt Chart

Sequence no.	Activity	May																													June				
		1	2	3	4	5	8	9	10	11	12	15	16	17	18	19	22	23	24	25	26	29	30	31	1	2	5	6	7	8					
1	Design change																																		
2	Prepare blueprints																																		
3	Purchase materials																																		
4	Manufacture parts																																		
	Frames																																		
	Flanges																																		
	Handles																																		
	Gears																																		
	Guides																																		
5	Assemble																																		
6	Paint																																		
7	Test																																		
8	Package																																		

Symbols:

Scheduled: ☐

Completed: ▨

Exercise 19.2—Inventory Control

PURPOSE

Help students gain a clearer understanding of inventory control, economic order quantity, and reorder point

TIME REQUIRED

45 minutes

    Step 1: Small-group activity (30 minutes)

    Step 2: Class discussion (15 minutes)

MATERIALS NEEDED

None

PROCEDURE

Step 1: The instructor will divide the class into small groups. Each group will: (1) review the inventory control material in the text, (2) solve The EOQ Problem (p. 225), and (3) solve The Reorder Point Problem (p. 227).

Step 2: A representative of each group will present the group's findings for class discussion.

The EOQ Problem

You are part of a project team that is trying to solve some of the company's inventory problems. Most of the inventory headaches have involved a critical relay with purchase only from one source and lead time for procurement of 30 days. The firm uses 10,000 of these relays a year in a steady, continuous manner. The relays cost $20 each, no matter how many are purchased at a time. According to the Cost Department, the setup cost is $120 every time a relay purchase order is processed, and inventory carrying costs run 10%, or $2 per unit.

Therefore,

$$R = \text{Annual Demand} = 10,000 \text{ Units}$$
$$P = \text{Price/Unit} = \$20$$
$$S = \text{Setup Cost/Order} = \$120$$
$$C = \text{Carrying Cost } (10\%) = \$2/\text{Unit}$$
$$LT = \text{Lead Time} = 30 \text{ Days}$$

Using the trial and error method, which of the following order sizes is best for the firm?

Order Size	Order Cost $(R/Q) \times (S)$	+	Carrying Cost $(Q/2) \times (C)$	=	Total Cost
10,000		+		=	
5,000		+		=	
2,000		+		=	
1,000		+		=	
500		+		=	

Using the Economic Order Quantity (EOQ) Formula, compute below the EOQ for the relays.

$$EOQ = \sqrt{\frac{2RS}{C}}$$

$$EOQ =$$

Check the EOQ answer with the trial and error method finding to be sure they are relatively close.

The Reorder Point Problem

The committee is reminded that the lead time for procurement for this relay is 30 days and that nothing can be done to expedite this procurement. Since the relays are needed every day in the factory, a stockout (zero inventory level) is very costly to the company. Therefore, you need to be sure that the orders are placed at the proper time. If done most efficiently, a new order of relays would be received on the day the last relay is issued from the old stock.

Assuming you begin the year with 1,000 relays in stock, at what point should a new order be placed? At what point should the second order be placed? And the following orders? Using the Inventory Control Chart, below, graph the usage and ordering of the relays. Note the Reorder Points and the Lead Times.

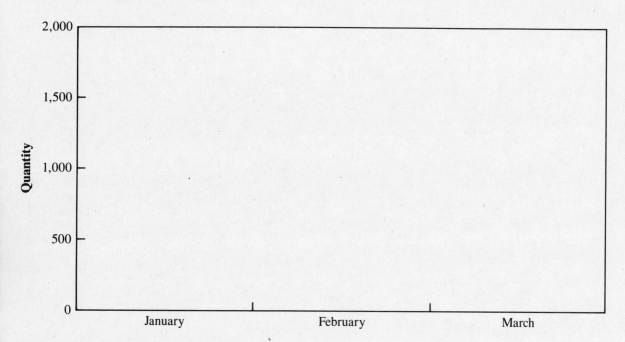

See the following logic for the above chart:

On hand as of January 1 = 1,000 units

Units used per year = 10,000 units

Units used per month = 10,000/12 = 833 units/month

Lead time = 30 days

Usage in that lead-time period = 833 units

Thus, when inventory reaches 833, send the new order, which should be received the day the last old relay is issued from stock.

Thus, 833 is the reorder point throughout the year.

CHAPTER 20   MANAGING TECHNOLOGY AND INNOVATION

Exercise 20.1—How to Improve the System

PURPOSE

Help students to understand the difficulties in designing a user-friendly automated service system

TIME REQUIRED

45–60 minutes

MATERIALS NEEDED

None

PROCEDURE

Step 1:   Students will be asked to select an automated service that they have had difficulty using. Some suggestions include automated tellers, automated 1-800 numbers, call-directing systems used by banks or schools, or touch-screen directories in stores.

Step 2:   Students will detail specific problems they encountered with their chosen systems and propose ways of remedying these problems.

Step 3:   Written plans for redesigned systems will be submitted and shared with the class.

Used with permission of Michele Kacmar, copyright © 1993.

Exercise 20.2—What Do You Make Out of This Junk?

PURPOSE

Help students develop skills in creative problem-solving through brainstorming

TIME REQUIRED

60–75 minutes

    Step 1: Small-group activity (40–60 minutes)

    Step 2: Class presentation (10–15 minutes)

    Step 3: Class discussion (open-ended)

PROCEDURE

Step 1:   Read the situation below.

SITUATION

You are an executive management team of Old News, Inc. Until recently, your company has been able to generate a substantial profit by producing and selling cellulose insulation for buildings. Your primary production materials have been old newspapers, purchased at low rates from recycling programs, and lock-top-style plastic bags. Recently, however, a new form of insulation has been sweeping the market, and you see your market share steadily decreasing.

You have several warehouses full of your basic materials and an ample and inexpensive supply of more of the same readily available. Your job is to come up with (1) a new product for your company to produce that uses both of these available materials, and (2) a name for your product.

Several management teams from Old News, Inc., have been assigned to brainstorm and come up with suggestions for the most marketable and most profitable product. There will be a large financial bonus for the group that comes up with the idea that is ultimately adopted.

Working with three to five of your classmates, assign a facilitator, and go through the six steps of the brainstorming process to find a product and then to decide on a name.

If you finish early, use the time to generate a backup concept in case your primary product proves to be impractical.

Step 2:   Report your decision to the class, and discuss the merits of each of the suggestions.

Step 3:   Class discussion.

Wohlberg, Janet W., *OB in Action* (Boston: Houghton Mifflin, 1992), p. 143. Copyright © 1992 by Houghton Mifflin Company. Used with permission.

QUESTIONS FOR DISCUSSION

1. What were the strengths and weaknesses of the brainstorming method?

2. In what kinds of situations would you use this method? In what kinds of situations would this method be inappropriate.

3. How did you feel during the process? Were you encouraged to participate? If not, what got in the way, and why? At any time, did you feel discounted? Why?

4. In what ways would you alter this process to make it more effective?

CHAPTER 21   MANAGING INFORMATION SYSTEMS

Exercise 21.1—Rumor Clinic: A Communications Experiment

PURPOSE

Illustrate distortions that may occur in transmission of information from an original source through several individuals to a final destination

TIME REQUIRED

30 minutes

MATERIALS NEEDED

Newsprint and a felt-tipped marker

PROCEDURE

Step 1:   The facilitator asks for six volunteers. (The rest of the group remains to act as process observers.)

Step 2:   Five of the six volunteers are asked to go into the isolation room. One remains in the meeting room with the facilitator and the observers.

Step 3:   The facilitator distributes Rumor-Clinic Observation Forms to the observers, who are to take notes on the proceedings.

Step 4:   He or she then reads the "accident report" on the Observation Form to the volunteer, who may not take notes on what he or she hears.

Step 5:   The facilitator asks a volunteer in the isolation room to return.

Step 6:   The first volunteer repeats to the second what he or she heard from the facilitator. *It is important that each volunteer transmit the message in his or her own way, without help.*

Step 7:   A third volunteer returns, and the second repeats what he or she heard from the first.

Step 8:   The process is repeated until all volunteers but the sixth have had the message transmitted to them.

Reprinted from: *A Handbook of Structured Experiences for Human Relations Training* [Vol. II], San Diego, CA: Pfeiffer & Company, 1974. Used with permission.

Step 9:   Then the sixth volunteer returns to the room. He or she is told that he or she is to assume the role of policeman. The fifth participant repeats the message to the policeman. Afterwards, the policeman writes the message on newsprint so the group can read it.

Step 10:   The facilitator then posts the original message (previously prepared on newsprint) so it can be compared with the policeman's version.

Step 11:   Observers are asked to report their notes. Volunteers then discuss their experience. The facilitator leads a discussion with the entire group on implications of the Rumor Clinic.

Rumor-Clinic Observation Form

Accident Report: "I cannot wait to report this accident to the police. I must get to the hospital as soon as possible.

"The delivery truck, heading south, was turning right at the intersection when the sports car, heading north, attempted to turn left. When they saw that they were turning into the same lane, they both honked their horns but continued to turn without slowing down. In fact, the sports car seemed to be accelerating just before the crash."

Volunteer	Additions	Deletions	Distortions
1			
2			
3			
4			
5			
6 (Policeman)			

Exercise 21.2—The New Ethics of Information Management

PURPOSE

Help students gain a new appreciation for the ethical issues being introduced by the technological advance of information systems

TIME REQUIRED

45 minutes

    Step 1: Small-group research activity (completed before class)

    Step 2: Class presentations and discussion (45 minutes)

MATERIALS NEEDED

None

PROCEDURE

Step 1: The instructor will divide the class into four groups and give each group one of the Ethical Issues in Information Management. The group is to go to the library and research the pros and cons (advantages and disadvantages) of that Ethical Issue and prepare a ten minute class presentation that will explain both its good and bad features. Each group member should have a role in the class presentation.

ETHICAL ISSUES IN INFORMATION MANAGEMENT

1. Computer "hackers" are able to tap into computers and data bases throughout the world and obtain and use that information.

2. Employers can use computers to "electronically" monitor the behavior of workers. For example, telephone-related computers can check numbers called and record names and addresses of parties called, the time of calls, and the politeness of conversation. Computers can monitor employee movements in firms that use coded cards to open doors.

3. The addition of robotics can make a firm more effective but create unemployment.

4. In the new "plastic" or "electronic money" society, people won't have to carry cash with them or worry about checks that bounce.

5. The new "electronic cottage" will provide work for those who may have difficulty getting to and from the office.

Step 2: Each group will make a ten minute class presentation on their Ethical Issue.

CHAPTER 22   MANAGING CULTURAL DIVERSITY

Exercise 22.1—What You See Isn't Necessarily What You Get

PURPOSE

Help students realize that we are all guilty to some degree of stereotyping, whether or not it is done consciously

TIME REQUIRED

About 45 minutes

Step 1: Individual evaluation (5–10 minutes)

Step 2: Small group discussions (10–20 minutes)

Step 3: Class discussion (15–20 minutes)

PROCEDURE

Step 1:   Read the situation below to yourself, and decide who it is that is standing at your door and why you believe it to be that person. Make some notes on the worksheet on p. 241 as to your rationale for eliminating the other possibilities and selecting the one that you did.

SITUATION

You have just checked into a hospital room for some minor surgery the next day. When you get to your room, you are told that the following people will be coming to speak with you within the next several hours:

1. The surgeon who will do the operation
2. A nurse
3. The secretary for the department of surgery
4. A representative of the company that supplies televisions to the hospital rooms
5. A technician who does laboratory tests
6. A hospital business manager
7. The dietician

You have never met any of these people before and don't know what to expect.

About half an hour after your arrival, a woman who seems to be of Asian ancestry appears at your door dressed in a straight red wool skirt, a pink-and-white-striped polyester blouse with a bow at the neck, and red medium-high heel shoes that match the skirt. She is wearing gold earrings, a gold chain necklace, a gold wedding band, and a white hospital laboratory coat. She is carrying a clipboard.

Wohlberg, Janet W., *OB in Action* (Boston: Houghton Mifflin, 1992), pp. 31–32. Copyright © 1992 by Houghton Mifflin Company. Used with permission.

Step 2: Working in small groups or with the class as a whole, discuss who might be standing at your door and why you believe it to be that person. In a place visible to all, reproduce the grid found with this exercise, and use it to record the responses of class members.

Step 3: In class discussion, consider the stereotypes used to reach a decision, and consider the following:

1. How hard was it to let go of your original decision once you had made it?

2. What implications do first impressions of people have about how you treat them, the expectations you have of them, and whether the acquaintance is likely to go beyond the initial stage?

3. What implications do your responses to the above questions have to the way you, as a manager, might treat a new employee? What will the impact be on that employee?

4. What are the implications for yourself in terms of job hunting and so forth?

QUESTIONS FOR DISCUSSION

1. Of the seven people listed, which of them is standing at your door? How did you reach this conclusion?

2. If the woman had not been wearing a white hospital laboratory coat, how might your perceptions of her have differed? Why?

3. If you find out that she is the surgeon who will be operating on you in the morning, and thought she was someone different initially, how confident do you now feel in her ability as a surgeon? Why?

What You See Isn't Necessarily What You Get

On the grid below, list the reasons that the woman standing before you is or is not each of the following individuals. Also, take a vote, and list the number of people in your class who select each possibility.

		Number who make this selection
Surgeon		
Nurse		
Secretary		
Television Representative		
Laboratory Technician		
Business Manager		
Dietician		

Exercise 22.2—The Kidney Transplant

PURPOSE

Help students recognize the difficulty of distinguishing between available "facts" and subjective feelings when making decisions affecting the lives of others

TIME REQUIRED

About 60 minutes

Step 1: Individual activity (15–20 minutes)

Step 2: Small-group decision making (30–40 minutes)

PROCEDURE

Step 1: Read the profiles on each of the transplant candidates and rank them from 1 to 5, with 1 being the patient you would give highest priority to for a transplant and 5 the lowest. Record the order on the Transplant Grid on p. 247.

SITUATION AND PROFILES

You are a member of the Ethics and Policy Committee of a medium-size urban hospital and teaching facility. Your committee is charged with making decisions about research proposals and innovative medical procedures. When resources are short, the committee must also decide which patients will receive special services. This last responsibility usually leaves you with the uncomfortable feeling that you are being asked to play God. You are painfully aware that many patients who are not selected for special services face almost certain death.

This is exactly the case before you now. Five patients in your hospital have been recommended by your hospital's kidney transplant team as having the physical and psychological stamina necessary for a transplant operation. Without transplants, *all* of them face about one hundred to one odds that they won't survive beyond another three months. In the five years that the transplant unit has been in place, kidneys have become available at an average of about four a year. At times, the unit has had to wait as long as four months for kidney availability. It is impossible to know just when a kidney will become available. When one does, it will be on such short notice that it is important to have decided in advance which patient will be the recipient. Because all of the patients are critically ill, it is conceivable that one or more may die before a kidney becomes available, or that one or more could develop complications from their disease that could render them unacceptable as transplant candidates. If either of these possibilities comes about for the individual who is number one on the priority list, your transplant team needs to know immediately which patient will be moved in to take his or her place. Because any number of the patients could become unacceptable, you need to establish the order in which you will consider the five patients for transplant.

The transplant team has given you histories on each of the patients, including their personal and family backgrounds. You must consider the information and make your decisions. Your committee should discuss each candidate and reach a consensus (based on discussion rather than voting) as to who will be first, second, third, fourth, and fifth in line for this life-saving operation.

Wohlberg, Janet W., *OB in Action* (Boston: Houghton Mifflin, 1992), pp. 37–40. Copyright © 1992 by Houghton Mifflin Company. Used with permission.

Sandra M., Age 34, Black, Baptist

Sandra is a registered nurse with three children, all under nine. She had worked the 11 P.M. to 7 A.M. shift at your hospital for six years until four months go when her illness became too severe. The money she had been earning, and her willingness to work the night-to-morning shift, allowed her husband, James, a full-time paralegal in a major law firm, to pursue a law degree at a local night law school. Over the past four months, James has had to stop his law school classes (in which he was consistently earning top grades) in order to care for Sandra and the children. During the day, home health aides come in to assist Sandra. James drops the youngest child off at day care and drives the two older children to school on his way to work. He leaves work at lunchtime to pick the older children up and take them to the day care provider, and in the evening he picks them up. There are few community support services available to the couple. Sandra is an only child whose parents had her rather late in life: both have been dead for over ten years. James has one married brother, but he lives in another city seven hundred miles away, as do his parents, who themselves are not well.

When Sandra and James were married almost a dozen years ago, they were full of high hopes. James had just graduated from a major university with a degree in business and had taken a job with the law firm, initially in their bookkeeping department. Sandra had graduated from the nursing school of the same university. They have both sung in their church choir, and Sandra had organized a support group for young mothers in their community.

Now Sandra is scared and depressed. She is increasingly upset with the realization that her illness has drained their young family both financially and emotionally, and she worries about her children and the impact her illness is having on them. Sandra prays that she will be considered to be a viable candidate for a kidney transplant so that she and James can continue to raise their family and share the love they feel so deeply for one another.

Sara Y., Age 42, White, Jewish

Sara is an English professor at Boston University. She is popular with students, has won the Metcalfe Award for Excellence in Teaching, and consistently has received highest evaluations for her courses. In addition, she is a member of the Democratic Women's Caucus and The League of Women Voters and is active in the Planned Parenthood Association (an organization that supports a woman's right to make choices about pregnancy, abortion, and birth control).

Last April, Sara received both good news and bad news on the same day: her first book won a national writers' award, and her kidney disease was diagnosed. She is currently on a semester leave as her illness has left her physically exhausted and unable to concentrate.

Sara grew up in a middle-class family in the Midwest. She received her undergraduate degree from an eastern women's college, a master's degree in English from Stanford, and just after she turned twenty-four, she settled into the role of housewife, having married her high school sweetheart. At age 29, she became a widow when her husband died in a plane crash. She was left with three young children. A substantial settlement from the airline allowed her to live comfortably, care for her children, and return to school for a Ph.D. in English literature, which she completed in five years. During her Ph.D. program, Sara met and married a Boston University history professor fifteen years her senior. A widower, he had four children, two of whom are now students at the university, a sophomore and a senior respectively. The oldest child has completed college and works in Vermont on an experimental farm; the youngest is still in high school. Sara's children are also still in high school. The couple adopted one another's children, creating what Sara calls "sort of a Jewish Brady Bunch." Sara's second husband died suddenly two years ago when he had a heart attack during his tenure hearings.

"My work isn't over," says Sara. "I know I'm not the only one in the world who can teach English and write books. That's something I do for me, something I feel good about. But I am the only one left for seven terrific kids, and they just don't deserve this."

Peter V., Age 27, White, No Religion Stated

Peter is a college dropout who has never held a steady job. His father, a member of your hospital's board of directors, has been particularly useful in helping the hospital weave its way through local red tape and politics. Peter's father also has been a major donor and an invaluable fundraiser. His efforts have been critical to the continued operation of the kidney transplant unit, which year after year incurs an enormous operating deficit and even now operates under the constant threat of being closed for lack of funds.

Unlike his very generous father, Peter behaves in an arrogant, demanding, and entitled manner. Since his admission to the hospital four months ago, he has angered and frustrated much of your staff. His nurse call button always seems to be on, but the nursing staff complains that when they respond, his demands are for channel changes on his television, pillow adjustments, and other petty requests. In addition, many members of the staff say they're uncomfortable with the steady stream of questionable characters who visit Peter's room night and day.

You have known Peter since he was a small child. He was a sweet boy, bright, fairhaired, and lively. At age thirteen, Peter was sent to the finest private boys' school in your area. You have heard rumors that Peter was suspended several times for drinking on school grounds or coming to classes drunk and that each time his father pressured the school to take him back. Ultimately he graduated, although you suspect he was given "social passes" to get him through and out without alienating his parents. Peter went on to a local two-year college, and for a time it looked like he was really going to straighten out. His parents have continued to support him since he dropped out of college at age twenty. They tell you that they will never abandon their son and that they believe that their love and support will ultimately bring him around. Until his admission to the hospital, Peter had been living in his parents' home.

Peter's father appears despondent over Peter's medical condition. Peter's mother, however, is angry and seems to hold the hospital responsible for every ache and pain her son is suffering. She has stated openly to members of her various clubs that if Peter does not receive a kidney, she and her husband will "stop all financial support and see to it that the hospital is made to pay for its negligence."

Chris J., Age 37, White, Methodist

Chris holds a Ph.D. in biology and worked on a research team at a leading biotech firm until two months ago when health complications made further work impossible. Scientists at the biotech firm believe that, thanks in large part to a major breakthrough by Chris, they are close to developing a drug intervention for use when AIDS is diagnosed at an early stage. Largely on the strength of Chris's work, the firm has been able to raise considerable capital and two government grants to continue the investigation and drug development. You've had a recent visit from the CEO of the biotech firm, a personal friend and former member of your hospital's staff, who came to plead on Chris's behalf. "Without Chris," the CEO told you, "we would not be as close to a cure for AIDS as we are. We're on the edge here of being able to save thousands of lives, and Chris is important to us."

Chris has been in a stable, same-sex "marriage" for thirteen years with Lee, a social worker for a local "safe house" for battered women. Chris and Lee have established a home in the suburbs, and Chris's elderly mother lives with them. (Chris's father was an alcoholic who disappeared when Chris was nine.) They have been active in their community, where they are socially popular and accepted by most, although by no means all, of their neighbors. A year ago Chris and Lee cochaired their community's successful Red Feather charity drive.

As a scientist, Chris is philosophical about the likelihood of a kidney transplant. "Life is so fragile and uncertain," says Chris. "I see that every day in the laboratory. I desperately want to live because I think I have a lot to contribute, but I also know that I could walk across the street and get hit by a car. Who ever knows?"

Cuong Ti D., Age 34, Asian, Catholic

Cuong came to the United States from Vietnam, where his parents, brother, and one of his two sisters had been killed by Vietcong snipers during a raid on his village. Cuong and his younger sister, an infant at the time, had escaped and hidden in the jungle for over a month before American soldiers found them and helped them to safety. Though only a young boy, Cuong had become invaluable to the U.S. troops for his knowledge of the strategically critical area surrounding his native village. He served as a guide on reconnaissance missions and successfully guided the American soldiers on eight such missions before he was captured. His captors took him to a North Vietnamese prison camp, where he was beaten and tortured for more than five years before he was able to escape. With the help of therapy, he has been able to gain some control over the nightmares he has suffered from these experiences.

Members of the Lutheran Church who sponsored his immigration to the United States are proud of Cuong's accomplishments. He studied English and, within a year, was accepted at a top university. He completed his undergraduate degree in engineering in three years on an army ROTC scholarship, while also holding a part-time job and keeping house for himself and his sister, who is, as far as he knows, his only surviving relative. After graduation, he took a full-time job, pursued and completed a master's degree in metallurgy at night, and continued to serve in the army reserves.

In late January 1991, Cuong was called into active service in Operation Desert Storm in Saudi Arabia. The doctors in charge of Cuong's case believe that his kidney damage was probably caused by the beatings he suffered in Vietnam but lay dormant until dehydration, suffered while in the Saudi Desert, brought his condition to where it is now.

For Cuong, life has just begun. Despite all he has been through, Cuong is optimistic. Two years ago, he met a Vietnamese woman whose story paralleled his own in many ways, and they have just recently become engaged. "God didn't bring me through all of this to let me die now," he told your staff psychiatrist. "I've been to hell and back—and I'm just not ready for a return trip."

Step 2:   Working in groups of five to seven students, discuss each of the patients and, as a group, rank the patients again from 1 to 5, again with 1 being the highest priority. Do this by reaching a consensus based on discussion, not by voting.

Transplant Grid

	Your Ranking	Group Ranking	Influence Score	Comments/Reasons
Sandra M.				
Sara Y.				
Peter V.				
Chris J.				
Cuong Ti D.				

CHAPTER 23   ENTREPRENEURSHIP AND NEW VENTURE FORMATION

Exercise 23.1—Starting a Small Business

PURPOSE

Help students understand the many complexities involved in starting a small business

TIME REQUIRED

45 minutes

    Step 1: Small-group research activity (completed before class)

    Step 2: Class discussion (45 minutes)

MATERIALS NEEDED

None

PROCEDURE

Step 1:   The instructor will divide the class into small groups and assign each group one of the following small business start-up opportunities:

1. Pet Store
2. Craft and Hobby Shop
3. Fast-Food Restaurant
4. Lawn Maintenance Service
5. Florist Shop
6. Yogurt Shop

    The group's task is to investigate the feasibility of that business opportunity in your geographic location, by completing The Small Business Situation Analysis (pp. 251–252). Students can find the needed information through library research or by interviewing people in similar businesses or in business advisory organizations, such as the U.S. Small Business Administration. Because there is so much research to do, different members may be assigned to do portions of it.

Step 2:   A group representative will present the group's findings for class discussion.

The Small Business Situation Analysis

1. Define the Market:

    a. What need does the product/service satisfy?_____
    _____
    _____
    _____

    b. How can our product/service be unique/better?_____
    _____
    _____
    _____

    c. Describe the customer that will buy this product/service._____
    _____
    _____
    _____
    _____

    d. How large is this market of customers?_____
    _____
    _____

    e. What is the projected growth rate of the market?_____
    _____
    _____

    f. What possible changes in the environment might affect this market?_____
    _____
    _____
    _____
    _____
    _____
    _____

2. Define the Competition:

   a. List the major competitors, identifying major strengths and weaknesses of each:_____

_____

_____

_____

_____

_____

_____

_____

_____

_____

_____

   b. Are there any unique market/industry characteristics, such as government regulations?_____

_____

_____

_____

_____

_____

_____

_____

_____

   c. Are there any unique market/industry success factors to consider?_____

_____

_____

_____

_____

_____

_____

Exercise 23.2—Should You Buy a Business or a Franchise?

PURPOSE

Help students understand the relative merits of buying an ongoing business or franchise

TIME REQUIRED

45 minutes

    Step 1: Small-group research activity (completed before class)

    Step 2: Class discussion (45 minutes)

MATERIALS NEEDED

None

PROCEDURE

Step 1: The instructor will divide the class into the same small groups used in Exercise 23.1.

  Reminder: In Exercise 23.1, each group was assigned to investigate one of the following small business opportunities:

1. Pet Store
2. Craft and Hobby Shop
3. Fast-Food Restaurant
4. Lawn Maintenance Service
5. Florist Shop
6. Yogurt Shop

    The group's task is to investigate the relative merits of buying an ongoing business or franchise in your area versus starting up a new one in your area, by completing The Ongoing Business Analysis (p. 255) and The Franchise Analysis (p. 257). Students can find the needed information through library research or by interviewing people in similar businesses or in business advisory organizations, such as the U.S. Small Business Administration. Because there is so much research to do, different members may be assigned to do different portions of it.

Step 2: A group representative(s) will present the group's findings for class discussion.

The Ongoing Business Analysis

Advantages of Buying an Ongoing Business: _____
_____
_____
_____
_____
_____
_____
_____
_____
_____
_____
_____
_____
_____
_____
_____
_____

Disadvantages of Buying an Ongoing Business: _____
_____
_____
_____
_____
_____
_____
_____
_____
_____
_____
_____
_____
_____
_____
_____
_____

The Franchise Analysis

Advantages of a Franchise: _____

_____

_____

_____

_____

_____

_____

_____

_____

_____

_____

_____

_____

_____

_____

_____

Disadvantages of a Franchise: _____

_____

_____

_____

_____

_____

_____

_____

_____

_____

_____

_____

_____

_____

_____

_____